ENDORSEMENTS

I count it a privilege to write the endorsement for the book "According to Your Word Lord, I Pray," for my dear friend, Louis McCall, which I feel will be a source of real blessing to each reader. I know that every chapter will relate the inspirational truths regarding knowing God in a more intimate way as He works demonstrating His power, purpose, favor, blessing, and provision in having faith in God and knowing the power of prayer.

There is no one more familiar after years of ministry and Christian experience, other than Louis McCall, to write the chapters of this book and convey their magnanimous truths. Each chapter will be a source of encouragement and strength to every reader as they point out that we must trust God and not be controlled by circumstances or uncertainties of life, but remain faithful to God's calling and His plan and purpose for our lives.

Rev. (Dr.) Huldah Buntain
President – Assemblies of God Mission
Calcutta, India
Author of *Pathway to the Impossible; Treasures in Heaven – the Personal Struggles and Private Victories of the Wife of India's Most Famous Modern Missionary;* and *A Quiet Escape: Moments to Replenish Your Soul.*

The book (According to Your Word Lord, I Pray) is thought provoking as the writer shares through Scripture who God is—His characteristics and attributes—and what that means to us as believers. Louis McCall shares his personal relationship with God based on His Word. It was inspiring.

DeVane McGee
Assemblies of God World Missions
Director of Development for Africa's Hope

Louis McCall is one who moves at God's word. When I entered Government as Ambassador at Large for International Religious Freedom, others were presenting me documents and briefings to read. Louis gave me the WORD, to hold me, to sustain me, to strengthen me. He has captured not only the essence of his own heart, but also God's in this book. I highly commend it to you. This is a man who lives what he preaches, and moves according to God's WORD.

Ambassador Suzan Johnson Cook
Author, FaithFeminist, Entrepreneur, Diplomat
God's Woman
Author of *Praying for the Man in Your Life; Balancing Your Life: God's Plan for Hope and a Future; Too Blessed to Be Stressed: Words of Wisdom for Women on the Move; Live Like You're Blessed: Simple Steps for Making Balance, Love, Energy, Spirit, Success, Encouragement, and Devotion Part of Your Life*; and other inspirational books.

Each of us has a lens that we see our world through. The lens, however, is grimed up with our past experiences and relationships. As a result, what we see around us is clouded. If we're going to experience the fullness of life that God intends for us, we need to wipe those lens clean. That's the experience of reading According to Your Word, I Pray. The negative experiences that have clouded your view of God, yourself and your relationship to Him will be wiped clean and replaced with Truth from God's Word. Dr. Louis uses a powerful prayer to organize a life's worth of learning from Scripture into one life-changing book. Set aside the time, soak in all this book has to offer and then hold it as a resource to keep coming back to. Your life will not be the same.

Harrison Wilder

Author of *The Honor Cycle: How to Go From Enduring Family to Enjoying Family.* www.harrisonwilder.com

According to Your Word Lord, I Pray is a powerful and well-written book that teaches the believer how to be an effective Christian. It is written by a man who prays and lives by the principles of which he writes. My husband, Onael Mdobilu, Senior Pastor of Manzese B Assembly of God Church in Dar es Salaam, Tanzania, and I have known Louis McCall for almost 14 years, since 2000 when, as a miraculous answer to prayer, God used him to arrange for our church to receive the finances we needed to buy land for a church building in a difficult and disadvantaged area. The church has since been thriving and now boasts of 500 members.

This wonderful book is also a manual that encourages Christians in their walk with God by opening their eyes to what their Heavenly Father has in store for them. "But as it is written, eye has not seen, nor ear heard, nor have entered into the heart of man, the things that God hath prepared for them that love him." (1 Corinthians 2:9) In it, one can find out how to communicate with and receive answers from a loving Heavenly Father and can discover that nothing can defeat the Word of God in the mouth of a believer because Jesus, the High Priest of our confession, is that very same Word.

Praying the word of God is releasing the power of God through our mouth—"Out of the mouths of babes and sucklings hast thou ordained strength, because of thine enemies, to silence the foe and the avenger" (Psalm 8:2)—and it helps us to challenge and bring change to the circumstances that life and the enemy of our souls would attack us with, something that we see through the pages of this excellent and educative book. Through this great work, Louis has done a wonderful job of showing the believer how to apply and benefit from the principles found in Scripture through prayer. I highly recommend it to the body of Christ and to anyone, anywhere who is seeking to make contact with the one true God of the Universe.

Justina Mdobilu
Co-Founder and Co-Pastor of Manzese B
Assembly of God Church, Dar es Salaam, Tanzania

According to Your Word Lord, I Pray

Louis A. McCall

According to Your Word Lord, I Pray

Secrets to Decree Your Future

Louis A. McCall

Advanced Global Publishing

P.O. Box 310, Shippensburg, PA 17257-0310

ISBN 13 TP: 978-0-7684-0727-3
For Worldwide Distribution
Printed in the U.S.A.

TABLE OF CONTENTS

ACKNOWLEDGEMENTS

I thank Holy Spirit God for impressing on me the need to write this book. I thank Him for helping me, teaching me, and revealing truths to me. I also owe a great debt to my wife Lenora for her patience, love, and encouragement. That this book has been birthed out is due in no small part to Lenora's perseverance with me in prayer to that end and a helpful reality check as needed.

The Holy Bible was my primary resource in producing this book. The spelling of the names of God and their associated scripture references were excerpted from *2031 Names of God: Transform Your Life as You Get to Know God in New Ways,* by Gaylyn Williams. Used by permission. wwww.2031namesoGod.com

INTRODUCTION

I'm always intrigued when I fly in an aircraft. While suspended between the earth and the heavens I let my mind take in the beauty as I gaze out my window, consider how great our creator God is, and how relatively insignificant the earth and I are in relation to the universe. (This was really driven home when, on July 19, 2013, the National Aeronautics and Space Administration took photographs of our tiny earth from the Messenger probe near Mercury and from the Cassini spacecraft near Saturn. Another famous photograph, taken by the Voyager 1 space probe in 1990 from beyond the boundary of our solar system, some 3.7 billion miles from earth, revealed an even smaller, pin prick-sized earth likened to a pale blue dot.) At such times I ponder the scripture

"What is man, that thou art mindful of him?" (Psalm 8:4)

So it was in May 2007, as I flew over the Caribbean Sea on my way home to Washington, D.C. from work-related business in Venezuela. Then it was I believe under inspiration from Holy Spirit God that I took a small note pad-sized sheet of paper and began to quickly pen two paragraphs. Those two paragraphs were simultaneously a prayer and a decree about my life. That was how it began. It lit a fire in me. Over the next six and a half years I added to that initial start as God revealed things to me in dreams or as God the Holy Spirit dropped rhema words and scriptures into my heart. In those times, I would delve into the study of the word of God to flesh out what had been revealed and to seek additional confirmation from Holy Scripture of what I intuitively knew God had placed in my heart. At times, I would share these with my dear wife Lenora. Mostly, I kept them to myself and pondered them in my heart during my personal devotions. Eventually, my decree became a lengthy one that was heavily footnoted with Bible references.

The word of God to the prophet Habakkuk was to "Write the vision, and make [it] plain upon tables, that he may run that readeth it." (Habakkuk 2:2) Thus, in a similar manner, I set about writing what was revealed to me in a way that people on the go, as they are in our time, could read it in plain understandable words as they go about their busy lifestyles. Perhaps you have seen people walking down the street or on public transportation, on their way somewhere, but still reading something on a smartphone, tablet, or other electronic device. For the most part they are reading something secular. It could be the news, a novel, the latest gossip on some entertainment personality, or it could be from a college text book, or the brief for a business meeting they are preparing for in order to be sharp and make a good impression. If this is done in secular life, then how much more is it not valid to do this with the things of God? God's instruction to His people, through His servant Moses, was to keep His words before you, using the memory refreshing devices of the day, and through vocal repetition to yourself and to your children.

"Therefore shall ye lay up these My words in your heart and in your soul, and bind them for a sign upon your hand, that they may be as frontlets between your eyes. And ye shall teach them your children, speaking of them when thou sittest in thine house, and when thou walkest by the way, when thou liest down, and when thou risest up." (Deuteronomy 11:18-19)

In short, keep your mind on the things of God and don't allow the press of life to crowd them out. The electronic devices of our day are memory aides. We don't have to know or memorize everything, we just need to know where to look it up and refresh our memories—and we are now able to do so on the go and at almost any time we wish.

As much as it was in me I would daily speak out loud the decree. If time did not permit me doing so with the full decree, I would focus on a small part, diving deep into associated scripture references. At that time, I was especially pleased with the revelations I received on the nature of God. These were not new revelations, but they were revelations to me in that I could see more clearly what I did not see before.

In those years, I went on many work-related overseas trips. Although I was a faithful employee focused on excellence, I also treated my personal time on those trips as spiritual retreats. They were opportunities to get alone with God and receive additional enlightenment. The time finally came for me to pull it together in a book, this book, that I believe will bless others. I implore the reader to use what follows, as I did and still do, to grasp the vision of who God is, our relationship with Him, and who we, as believers, are in Christ, notwithstanding the contradictory, lying claims of the world and our adversary the devil.

Some parts of the decree that this book focuses on are very personal in that they relate specifically to me, that is to Louis. Perhaps you may read those portions and identify with them saying "me too!" However, I encourage the reader to re-write those segments and personalize them to one's own situation.

In this book I honor God by capitalizing His proper name, names, and pronouns related to Him. I reserve the lower case format for the proper name, names, and pronouns related to the rebellious fallen angel we know as the devil. However, I do this only in my own narrative. Bible quotations are reproduced as they appear in the Bible without modifying the standard conventions for proper names and pronouns.

Bible quotations are from the King James Version, unless otherwise indicated. This book is organized so that all of the scripture references drawn upon are available for more intense study, but not all are quoted fully in the narrative for the sake of concision and readability. Bible quotations are given to allow the reader to see the foundation in holy writ for the confident decrees that are the cornerstone of this book. Unlike many other books, there is no effort given to a detailed expository run through of each portion of scripture cited.

CHAPTER 1
THE PRAYERFUL DECREE

The prayerful decree in this book is based on the word of God and should be spoken out loud. The word of God is the revealed will of God. When we pray, in faith, according to the will of God, by praying God's word as handed down to us in the scriptures, God hears and answers.

> *"And this is the confidence that we have in him, that, if we ask any thing according to his will, he heareth us: and if we know that he hear us, whatsoever we ask, we know that we have the petitions that we desired of him."* (1 John 5:14-15)

Speaking and hearing God's word, which is His will, is used in tandem with praying and decreeing His word out loud to get the results God desires that we experience. According to Romans 10:17, faith comes by hearing—hearing the word of God. The apostles prayed in Acts 4:29 that they would speak God's word with boldness. God's instruction, by Moses to his people in Deuteronomy 11:18-19, was that they put God's word in their hearts, teach them to their children, and speak those words at home, as they went about outside the home, when they laid down to sleep, and when they rose again the next day. God's word and will, through speaking it, hearing it, meditating upon it, and living our lives by it, is to be an integral part of all aspects of our lives. Although there are times to be silent in God's presence, the Bible speaks more often of lifting up our

1

voices in a joyful declaration of praises to God and recounting the goodness of God's character, His deeds on our behalf, and all of His promises that He delivers on that increase our faith and stir us to give testimony of His amazing greatness. "Let the redeemed of the Lord say so" is the command found in Psalm 107:2. There may be times for quiet meditation and thought, but as good as those times are more often the believer is commanded to give voice to the will of God and thereby align himself with God and activate his faith in the unfailing promises of God.

"And in that day shall ye say, Praise the LORD, call upon his name, declare his doings among the people, make mention that his name is exalted. Sing unto the LORD; for he hath done excellent things: this is known in all the earth. Cry out and shout, thou inhabitant of Zion: for great is the Holy One of Israel in the midst of thee." (Isaiah 12:4-6)

"To the end that my glory may sing praise to thee, and not be silent. O LORD my God, I will give thanks unto thee for ever." (Psalm 30:12)

This is not hypocrisy or delusion, rather it is faith

When I pray using the decree in this book I speak it out loud using my mouth and my faith. I do so in the spirit of Romans 4:17-18 that calls some things in my life that honestly do not yet fully exist in the eyes of third persons observing me, as though they were already apparent and manifested. Between the two persons that matter, that is between God and me, they do exist. This is not hypocrisy or delusion, rather it is faith. The apostle Paul wrote in his letter to the Romans that there is no need to have faith and hope for something that everyone, including unbelievers and detractors, can already see. What I do pray for does come into being, sometimes immediately, and sometimes after a period of time. I am also still waiting in faith for some things to come into being in the physical now that I experience from day to day as long as I live in my natural body.

"For we are saved by hope: but hope that is seen is not hope: for what a man seeth, why doth he yet hope for? But if we hope for that we see not, then do we with patience wait for it." (Romans 8:24:25)

"Now faith is the substance of things hoped for, the evidence of things not seen." (Hebrews 11:1).

Although I pray out loud using my faith, I also have substance and evidence that will stand in the court of heaven. Since Hebrews 11:6 informs us that God is only pleased by faith, I cannot allow myself the luxury or timidity of second guessing the word of God. Neither can you. I call on the reader to boldly make the decrees that follow and to do that out loud. Then, as the apostle Paul declared in 2 Corinthians 5:7, let us "walk by faith, not by sight."

Without Jesus I can do nothing

My mouth is teamed together with my mental assent and conception of my desired future state in this life to perfect my faith. As Romans 10:8-10 says "...with the mouth confession is made unto salvation." Just as speaking out with our mouths, paired with our hearts in believing the promises of God, jointly result in obtaining the reality of our salvation paid for by Jesus on our behalf, so too our active mouths, again paired with our hearts, work together in creating in our lives on earth all that Jesus said was our inheritance in Him.

Revelation 21:8 tells us that it is the fearful and unbelieving that have their place in the lake of fire, along with a list of other unsavory characters. So I use the God ordained and gifted faith given to every person, together with my mouth, to boldly speak out the reality of the promises of God, without fear or unbelief. I urge you to do the same. When we do so and begin to walk in that by the power of the blood of Jesus and of God the Holy Spirit, we will overcome and the lives we live on earth will catch up with our confessions. This is what happened when you felt sorry for your sins, turned from them, and confessed Jesus as your Lord and Savior while believing in your heart all that God's word says of Him.

I want to plainly state here that I am a very ordinary person. I am not putting myself on a pedestal. In John 15:5, Jesus gave the metaphor of a vine from which its branches receive life. I acknowledge the truth spoken by my Lord that without Jesus I can do nothing. Also, I identify with the apostle Paul on the matter of where I am now and what I am attempting to attain.

Make the decrees that follow...out loud

"Not as though I had already attained, either were already perfect: but I follow after, if that I may apprehend that for which also I am apprehended of Christ Jesus. Brethren, I count not myself to have apprehended: but this one thing I do, forgetting those things which are behind, and reaching forth unto those things which are before, I press toward the mark for the prize of the high calling of God in Christ Jesus." (Philippians 3:12-14)

The prayer that follows is also a decree, a prayerful decree. That is what this book is all about. Although it is my personal prayer, you can make it your own prayer too and tweak it, where necessary, to more closely fit with your own personal challenges and desires. In subsequent chapters I will break down the decree sentence by sentence and, in some instances, phrase by phrase or, when necessary, word by word. Join with me in this prayer of decree, based on God's word, and experience a new realm of relationship, power, and purpose in your daily walk with God.

The prayer immediately follows, is footnoted and, in its digital form, hyperlinked to the full form of selected scriptures, to facilitate easy reference and detailed study. Each subsequent chapter keys on successive sub-headings of the prayer, repeating in italics that portion of the prayer and then proceeding to break it down and provide appropriate select Bible references in a step-by-step process.

The Prayerful Decree

Who God Is and Who I Am In Him

God my Father, Abba, holy is Your name.[1] You are El Olam, the everlasting God,[2] the I AM[3] and I call on You[4] to remember Your promises in which You have caused me to hope.[5] Because of what Jesus did I am an heir of the covenant of blood and grace, by faith, that You made with Abraham, the father of the faithful.[6] As with Abraham, You have called me friend.[7] I am a son, a joint heir with Christ Jesus[8] and a child of El Elyon, the Most High God.[9] I am of the god-class of being and have been redeemed back to that status by the work of Christ Jesus.[10] I am not of this world system, but rather I am an ambassador[11] of the Kingdom of God and Your system of government in the earth.[12] I am of the royal priesthood,[13] a minister of God,[14] so that Your will is done on earth as it is in heaven.[15] I partner with God as a watchman.[16] When His Spirit seeks for a man I am available and I make up the hedge.[17] I prophesy all that the Lord says for me to declare.[18] I work the works of God.[19] I pray without ceasing[20] and my righteous prayers have power with God.[21]

I Know and Extol the Nature and Ways of God

I don't doubt the Word of God or His nature. The essence of His character is that He is good, peaceful, true, compassionate, kind, long-suffering, willing, excellent, pure, honorable, virtuous, Divine, venerable, adorable, holy, righteous, perfect, light, spirit, invisible, existential, glorious, splendorous, beautiful, unchanging, ineffable, incomparable, limitless, boundless, omnipresent, worthy, trustworthy, discerning, knowing, omniscient, understanding, humble, great, the head, transcendent, supreme, most high, Alpha and Omega, ancient of days, eternal, immortal, sovereign, majestic, wise, gentle, faithful, merciful, gracious, just, wonderful, benevolent, beneficent, passionate, and loving.

His nature in His works is marvelous, miraculous, mighty, almighty, omnipotent, awesome, creative, life-giving, powerful, redeeming, saving, all conquering, victorious, planning, and working.

His nature in His emotional feeling is joyous, jealous, furious, tender, and suffering.

His nature in His functions is judging, governing, ruling, avenging, prophetic, interceding, reconciling, high priest, savior, Lamb of God, redeemer, Christ, Messiah, author and finisher of our faith.

His nature in His relations is Lord, Master, Father, bridegroom, kinsman-redeemer, brother, Emmanuel, approachable, friendly, caring, nurturing, comforting, healing, beckoning, longsuffering, selfless, forgiving, counseling, sharing, serving, advocating, and mediating.

His nature in His assistance to and development of man is covenanting, leading, guiding, shepherding, correcting, chastening, reproving, consuming fire, directing, warring, liberating, delivering, saving, sheltering, protecting, shielding, keeping, purifying, refining, pruning, transforming, regenerating, enlightening, teaching, revealing, warning, pleading, trying, searching, renewing, restoring, sanctifying, perfecting, anointing, strengthening, befriending, satisfying, rewarding, promoting, exalting, favoring, prospering, blessing, and bountiful.

His indispensable being is the living Bread of Life, drink, living water, living Word, the way, the door, the life, and the light. This is the nature of God my Father who is light and the Father of lights.[22] The Father Himself loves me.[23] Jesus, the good shepherd, loves me and gave Himself for me.[24] The Holy Spirit, the Helper,[25] whom I do not grieve,[26] sticks closer to me than a brother, abides in me, teaches me all things, and anoints me to do the works of God and to destroy the works of the devil.[27]

I Am Sanctified by the Work of God and I Abide in Him

Lord, I seek your face, heart, and voice, and I find You.[28] I see the Lord.[29] I linger with You in Your glory light and am transformed into Your image as all within me that is not like You is consumed by the light of your glory and your holy fire.[30] I am a man after God's own heart.[31] I am a worshipper and have found the key of David that opens a door into the throne room of the manifest presence of God.[32] By Your grace and power Yahweh Mikkadesh, God my sanctifier,[33] I commit to keeping Your commandments,[34] doing all Your will,[35] and to walking in Jesus' commandment of love.[36] I pledge obedience and singleness of heart.[37] My old life and selfish, prideful, errant nature is crucified with Christ.[38] It is no longer I that live, but Christ.[39] The ideal servant of the Lord is reproduced in me.[40] I am washed in the Blood of Jesus from all sin and condemnation and I walk continually in holiness by the power of the Holy Ghost.[41] I consecrate myself to and abide in God[42] and revel in the ecstasy of His intimate presence.[43] Yahweh Shammah, the Lord is present,[44] is with me. I am kept clean daily by self-examination, the renewing of my mind,[45] and the washing of the water of the Word of God.[46] I take captive every thought that attempts to exalt itself above the knowledge of Christ.[47] I do not sin with my eyes; I flee from evil, I renounce ungodly soul ties and affections, and I do not dwell in places of unrighteousness. I do not consider, meditate upon, or act out ungodly pleasure.[48] No ungodly addiction has control of me, and when the prince of this world comes he finds no place in me.[49]

I Am a Wholly Devoted Follower of Christ Jesus

Jesus is El Yeshuati and Yahweh Shua, the God of my salvation and redemption.[50] I unreservedly believe and follow the revelation God my Father gave of Himself through the manifestation in human flesh of the person of Jesus. There is salvation in none other. As a true disciple of Christ Jesus, I take up my cross, in disregard of self-will, and follow Him.[51] I am strong in the LORD and of good courage.[52] Jesus is Yahweh Shalom, the Lord our peace.[53] I have the peace of God.[54] I do not fear man or the principalities and powers of satan's kingdom.[55] I am in reverential awe of God.[56] I don't halt between two opinions or vacillate between going God's way and trying to obtain success by going man's way.[57]

I Proclaim the Whole, True Gospel of the Person and Work of Christ Jesus

I boldly and effectively proclaim to the nations[58] the name of the LORD and His good news that the Kingdom of God is near, that we have entrance by faith through repentance from sin and by confession of and belief in the person and work of Christ Jesus,[59] His sin atoning shed blood, His substitutionary death on the cross, His resurrection, and the indwelling of the Holy Spirit, by which things we are saved from the kingdom of darkness, reconciled to God by His work of grace, and restored to our original and rightful places as His children, heirs of His Kingdom, and as co-rulers of the earth.[60]

I Engage in Spiritual Warfare and Conquer Through God

The power of witchcraft, demonic strongholds, curses, and of the curse over my life is broken, because Jesus took the curse on Himself that I would have the Blessing.[61] You are Yahweh Eloheka, the God who brings me out of slavery[62] and I stand fast in that liberty.[63] Jesus is Yahweh Nissi, God my banner – the Lord is my victory[64] and Yahweh Sabaoth, the Lord of angelic heavenly armies.[65] I resist the devil and he flees.[66] I bind and cast down to the pit demonic strongmen, spiritual principalities, and rulers of darkness in high places.[67] I restore the foundations, repair breaches, and build up God ordained walls to keep out the enemies of our souls.[68] I bring the light of God where there was darkness and deliver many from the bondage of captivity to life in the light and freedom of the Kingdom of God.[69] In my life and in the lives of others whose souls have been scared by others or by our own wrong choices and habits, I, by the Spirit of God, bring recovery of that which was damaged or stolen, deliverance from enslavement, and the gifts of restoration, healing, and reconciliation.[70] I am more than a conqueror through Him that loved me.[71]

You are Yahweh Elohay, the Lord my God who cares for me.[72] Nothing shall separate me from the love of Christ.[73] I rule and reign with Christ now, in this time, and in the ages to come.[74] My enemies are defeated whether they be in the flesh or from the spirit realm.[75] The devil, his demons, the kingdom of darkness, and the world system are defeated.[76] The power of sin and of condemnation over my life and destiny is broken.[77] In the power and authority of Jesus name I speak to the mountains of debt, diabetes, back problems, and excess weight and command them to go![78] Debt is defeated and cancelled.[79] Lack and the spirit of poverty are defeated.[80] The devourer is rebuked.[81] The thief is defeated.[82] You are Yahweh Rophe, God my healer, therefore diabetes, obesity, arthritis, allergies, back problems, and all sicknesses are defeated.[83] I bind and take authority over all the power of the enemy in Jesus' name.[84] You are Yahweh Gmolah, the Lord of recompense who rewards and compensates Your children.[85] You restore all that has been stolen from me and give me a recompense of double that which was stolen.[86] Your justice, when the thief is caught, restores to me seven times what was stolen.[87]

I Have God's Favor, Blessing, Provision, and Joy

I am made the righteousness of God, Yahweh Tsidkenu, in Christ Jesus.[88] My name is written in the Lamb's *Book of Life*.[89] Increase, favor, and the Blessing are mine.[90] I have access into the manifest presence of God on a spirit to Spirit basis.[91] I boldly ascend and enter into the throne room of the glory to worship God and then receive and bring into my world those revelations and gifts needful to establishing the dominion of God's Kingdom on earth.[92] I command a window in heaven to be opened over me through which angels ascend and descend with my heavenly Father's provision for me.[93] I loose my blessings and wealth from the blocking of delaying, hindering spirits and command money and good things to come to me now.[94] Good things: riches, money, favor, grace, wisdom, peace, joy, life, blessings, enriching ideas received and implemented, success, prosperity, God's manifest presence, and His ministering holy angels are all attracted to me.[95] People give me advantages, preferential treatment, favor, money, and beneficial things.[96] The wealth of the wicked and the hidden treasures of darkness are laid up for me.[97] God gives me witty inventions to patent and by which to profit.[98] God takes pleasure in blessing me with wealth to establish His covenant, and

I honor Adonai, the Lord my master, with my substance.[99] I have plenty because You are Yahweh Jireh, the Lord my provider who sees my needs and supplies where there was lack.[100] My cup of blessing overflows.[101] I have all that I desire and my joy is full.[102] My Lord is the God of all joy[103] and He bids me to enter into His joy.[104] The joy of the Lord is my strength.[105] He causes me to laugh with joy because of His salvation, redemption, deliverance, victory, blessing, and His word.[106]

I Live Out the Purpose of Blessing and Equipping in My Life

I go about doing good and operate in the gifts of the anointing.[107] I excel in the grace of giving, giving at the level I conceive and determine in my heart.[108] I establish and extend the Kingdom of God wherever I go.[109] I lift up and proclaim the name of Jesus; very God who humbled Himself, came down from heaven in the likeness and limitations of man by a virgin birth as a helpless baby, was crucified in the flesh in payment for the sins of the world, and is risen from the dead, so that men are drawn to Him and are saved.[110] By Him I bear much fruit and it is fruit that remains.[111]

I Am a Sower Who Imitates God

I am a blessing to others to the glory of God.[112] I am generous and I abound to every good work as I am led by the Spirit of Yahweh Rohi, God my shepherd.[113] Almighty God my satisfier and supplier, El Shaddai, gives me seed to sow and multiplies my seed sown.[114] I sow into good soil and reap a hundredfold return.[115] I sow many types of good seed and receive the sure harvests of my expectations and the assignments of those seeds.[116] I nurture the fatherless.[117] I give and keep giving to the poor, widows, and orphans, and God blesses me all the more.[118]

I Demonstrate the Power of the Spoken Word of Faith in Partnership with Holy Spirit God

I guard my heart and my mouth.[119] I do not sin with my words.[120] I speak life.[121] My spoken words contain and release the power of my faith in the immutable promises of God.[122] The sword of the Spirit is a powerful weapon wielded by my mouth.[123] By the Spirit of Christ and the Word spoken in faith, I deliver and set captives free, break chains that bind, remit the sins of those who have sinned against me,[124] and undo heavy burdens.[125] I pull down strongholds.[126] The gates of hell and its counsels shall not prevail.[127] As God's ambassador and a citizen of the Kingdom of God, Elohim, God the creator's Word in my mouth is as powerful as His Word spoken by His mouth.[128] So shall my word be that goes forth out of my mouth; it shall accomplish that which I please and shall be successful in the matter to which I assign it.[129] I request of God my Father and He dispatches ministering spirits.[130] They are more and stronger that be with me than those that come against me and the Kingdom of God.[131] The holy angels of God minister to me.[132] They harken to the voice of God's Word that I speak with faith, and God directs them to perform it.[133] I believe that I receive.[134] Life is in the power of my tongue. I love it and eat the fruit of it.[135] I have what I say.[136] I see it with the eye of faith and the images I conceive and meditate upon in my thoughts are established and manifested in this realm as in heaven.[137] I agree with the Word of God.[138] I obtain the promises of God.[139]

I Call Specific Personal Desires into Existence

I take hold of my inheritance.[140]

My Time, My Personal Calling, Mission, and Assignments

My set time and the seasons of my visitation have arrived.[141] God has made me to be a king in the marketplace and has given me money with a mission; prosperity with a purpose.[142] I am a multi-millionaire many times over.[143] I have the resources and use them to build and run orphanages to care for orphaned children,[144] raise them to know and receive Christ, and to raise up Christian workers from them; to build and run housing for seniors, the poor, widows, and the disabled, that include chapels, offer Bible studies, and provide for organized intercessory prayer.[145] And I have all kinds of profits from real estate investments in general. I develop and patent a breakthrough device and receive great wealth from fees and royalties. I fund and dispatch ministry and healing teams.[146] I am a forerunner for international evangelistic campaigns.[147] I heal and minister deliverance by the Spirit of Yahweh Rophe, God my healer.[148] I sing, compose, play Christian music, and write Christian books like *The Epic of God* and *According to Your Word Lord, I Pray*.[149] I support witnesses, and their families, who do not fear persecution and who are prepared to become martyrs for the sake of the gospel by refusing to be spared by denying Christ.[150] I give generously to every good work yet I am not diminished.[151]

I Ask and then Thank God for What Has Been Confessed As Already Done

I decree these things and they are established![152] I ask You, God my Father, to grant my petitions and to bring my words to pass.[153] I ask this of You in Jesus' name, the Apostle and High Priest of my confession.[154] I thank you God my Father, Abba, Daddy, that it is done, settled, established, and a present reality in my life on earth as it is in heaven. Amen.[155]

Chapter 2
Who God Is and Who
I Am In Him

God my Father, Abba, holy is Your name. You are El Olam, the everlasting God, the I AM and I call on You to remember Your promises in which You have caused me to hope. Because of what Jesus did I am an heir of the covenant of blood and grace, by faith, that You made with Abraham, the father of the faithful. As with Abraham, You have called me friend. I am a son, a joint heir with Christ Jesus and a child of El Elyon, the Most High God. I am of the god-class of being and have been redeemed back to that status by the work of Christ Jesus. I am not of this world system, but rather I am an ambassador of the Kingdom of God and Your system of government in the earth. I am of the royal priesthood, a minister of God, so that Your will is done on earth as it is in heaven. I partner with God as a watchman. When His Spirit seeks for a man I am available and I make up the hedge. I prophesy all that the Lord says for me to declare. I work the works of God. I pray without ceasing and my righteous prayers have power with God.

Knowing God

God my Father, Abba, holy is Your name. When the disciples asked Jesus to teach them to pray He instructed them to approach God as their Father and to hold His name holy and reverenced. I remember the first time I heard someone pray saying "My Father." I took immediate notice. I was convicted that this man before me prayed like Jesus. In those simple words he demonstrated a personal relationship with God his Father, that I realized I didn't have to that depth, but wanted.

> *"And he said unto them, When ye pray, say, Our Father which*
> *art in heaven, Hallowed be thy name."* (Luke 11:2)

You are El Olam, the everlasting God, the I AM and I call on You to remember Your promises in which You have caused me to hope. This book uses some of the many names of God. Some are not familiar to most readers, but all are from the Holy Bible. I have tried to give the reader the actual Hebrew or Greek rendering of those names as found in the original Bible text rather than just their meanings as Bible translators have translated them into English. These names help me to appreciate the many facets of our great God and to see Him better for all that He is. I meditate on the truth in His names and worship Him in holy awe.

> *"Hast thou not heard, [that] the everlasting God, the LORD,*
> *the Creator of the ends of the earth, fainteth not, neither is*
> *weary? [There is] no searching of his understanding."* (Isaiah
> 40:28)

God first revealed Himself as I AM when Moses asked who he should say had sent him (Exodus 3:13-15). Because He is God, and there is none greater, I take His many promises to us as irrefutable. God my Father even wants me to call out to Him and put Him in remberance of His promises.

> *"Then shall ye call upon me, and ye shall go and pray unto*
> *me, and I will hearken unto you."* (Jeremiah 29:12)

"Put me in remembrance: let us plead together: declare thou, that thou mayest be justified." (Isaiah 43:26)

It is not that He has a failing memory, but that he wants me to boldly approach Him as His child and let Him know that I am standing in faith on those promises.

"Remember the word unto thy servant, upon which thou hast caused me to hope." (Psalm 119:49).

The Bible is filled with promises of God that show His goodness and grace toward us. They are too many to list here in their entirety, but I have presented below a selection of those that have great significance for me.

"For all the promises of God in him [are] yea, and in him Amen, unto the glory of God by us." (2 Corinthians 1:20)

"God [is] not a man, that he should lie; neither the son of man, that he should repent: hath he said, and shall he not do [it]? or hath he spoken, and shall he not make it good?" (Numbers 23:19)

"Call unto me, and I will answer thee, and shew thee great and mighty things, which thou knowest not." (Jeremiah 33:3)

"For God so loved the world, that he gave his only begotten Son, that whosoever believeth in him should not perish, but have everlasting life." (John 3:16)

"Christ hath redeemed us from the curse of the law, being made a curse for us: for it is written, Cursed [is] every one that hangeth on a tree: that the blessing of Abraham might come on the Gentiles through Jesus Christ; that we might receive the promise of the Spirit through faith." (Galatians 3:13-14)

"If my people, which are called by my name, shall humble themselves, and pray, and seek my face, and turn from their wicked ways; then will I hear from heaven, and will forgive their sin, and will heal their land." (2 Chronicles 7:14)

"Verily, verily, I say unto you, he that believeth on me, the works that I do shall he do also; and greater [works] than these shall he do; because I go unto my Father. And whatsoever ye shall ask in my name, that will I do, that the Father may be glorified in the Son. If ye shall ask any thing in my name, I will do [it]." (John 14:12-14)

My Place in God

Because of what Jesus did I am an heir of the covenant of blood and grace, by faith, that You made with Abraham, the father of the faithful. I am in Christ Jesus and am a beneficiary of all He has provided through His covenant of blood and grace, which I enter into by faith, as did Abraham.

"And if ye [be] Christ's, then are ye Abraham's seed, and heirs according to the promise." (Galatians 3:29)

As with Abraham, You have called me friend. I have entered into a relationship of fellowship with the Godhead. As amazing as it is to contemplate, God calls me His friend just as Abraham was known as God's friend.

"Greater love hath no man than this, that a man lay down his life for his friends. Ye are my friends, if ye do whatsoever I command you. Henceforth I call you not servants; for the serant knoweth not what his lord doeth: but I have called you friends; for all things that I have heard of my Father I have made known unto you." (John 15:13-15)

The Godhead embraces me as an intimate

I am a son, a joint heir with Christ Jesus and a child of El Elyon, the Most High God. I have been adopted into the family of God as an heir alongside Christ Jesus with all of the rights and privileges pertaining to a son and an heir. As the scripture below indicates, the triune family of the Godhead embraces me as an intimate and envelopes me in the glory of God the most high.

> *"For as many as are led by the Spirit of God, they are the sons of God. For ye have not received the spirit of bondage again to fear; but ye have received the Spirit of adoption, whereby we cry, Abba, Father. The Spirit itself beareth witness with our spirit, that we are the children of God: and if children, then heirs; heirs of God, and joint-heirs with Christ; if so be that we suffer with [him], that we may be also glorified together."* (Romans 8:14-17)

I am of the god-class of being and have been redeemed back to that status by the work of Christ Jesus. When God created man He created man in His own image and likeness and gave him dominion over the earth, effectively making man the god of this world. Through sin, Adam, the first man, alienated mankind from God and turned over to satan the title of god of this world. Thus satan was within his power when he tempted Jesus with an easy path to the kingdoms of the earth. However, the death of Jesus as the sinless Lamb of God for the sins of the world, and His resurrection, ensured that all who believe on Jesus are restored to the status of sons of God and share with Jesus, who is fully God and fully man, in ruling the earth.

Operating at the level of the god-class of being

Even before Jesus came to redeem mankind we were given glimpses of man operating at the level of the god-class of being. God told Moses that He would make Moses a god to Pharaoh. Now the Pharaoh was a man who fancied himself to be a god until his fateful conflict with the only God and his chosen instrument Moses operating at the level of the god-class of being. Likewise, when Joshua commanded the sun to stand still until he finished the utter defeat of his enemy, there was a demonstration of what a man operating at the god-class level could do with the backing of God. The Acts of the Apostles demonstrated the promise of the resurrected Christ that believers would be able to do the things He did. They operated at the level of the god-class of being. The exciting thing is that more is to come. The Spirit of God is not finished with the work of honoring God the Son by anointing the sons and daughters of God, who believe on Jesus and walk in the Spirit, to operate in this life in the power and demonstration of the redeemed god-class of being. Jesus Himself, during His earthly ministry, confirmed the scripture that said we were gods, and He called for believers in Him to operate with the faith and results of that level. Although it stretches my faith, I strive, by the power and promises of God, to walk in the god-class to His glory.

> *"Jesus answered them, Is it not written in your law, I said, Ye are gods? If he called them gods, unto whom the word of God came, and the scripture cannot be broken; Say ye of him, whom the Father hath sanctified, and sent into the world, Thou blasphemest; because I said, I am the Son of God?"* (John 10:34-36)

> *"And Jesus answering saith to them, 'Have faith of God; for verily I say to you, that whoever may say to this mount, Be taken up, and be cast into the sea, and may not doubt in his heart, but may believe that the things that he saith do come to pass, it shall be to him whatever he may say. Because of this I say to you, all whatever -- praying -- ye do ask, believe that ye receive, and it shall be to you."* (Mark 11:22-24 Young's Literal Translation)

It is not that I can do anything of myself, and I certainly am not equal to God, but God Himself is in me and desires that His fullness be demonstrated on earth through the manifestation of Himself working through my flesh and blood body.

> *"That he would grant you, according to the riches of his glory, to be strengthened with might by his Spirit in the inner man; that Christ may dwell in your hearts by faith; that ye, being rooted and grounded in love, may be able to comprehend with all saints what [is] the breadth, and length, and depth, and height; and to know the love of Christ, which passeth knowledge, that ye might be filled with all the fullness of God."* (Ephesians 3:16-19)

> *"According as his divine power hath given unto us all things that pertain unto life and godliness, through the knowledge of him that hath called us to glory and virtue: whereby are given unto us exceeding great and precious promises: that by these ye might be partakers of the divine nature, having escaped the corruption that is in the world through lust."* (2 Peter 1:3-4)

I am not of this world system, but rather I am an ambassador of the Kingdom of God and Your system of government in the earth. The history of God's interaction with man repeatedly has God calling individuals out of what they knew, a world in rebellion and far from God's ways, to be His representatives and spokespersons with the task of warning their world to turn from its wayward path and the consequences of divine judgment. I have held diplomatic and consular titles in the service of the government of the United States of America. My first ambassador, who became a mentor and lifelong friend, impressed upon me that I was not just Louis, but that my position and words carried the weight and backing of the United States. The point he was making was that I could never separate myself from that fact while on assignment in a foreign country, and so I needed to comport myself and choose my words accordingly.

> *"Now then we are ambassadors for Christ, as though God did beseech [you] by us: we pray [you] in Christ's stead, be ye reconciled to God."* (2 Corinthians 5:20)

I am of the royal priesthood, a minister of God, so that Your will is done on earth as it is in heaven. I am not making myself bigger than I am, rather God has made me much bigger than the life I was living before I came into relationship with Him.

> *"But ye [are] a chosen generation, a royal priesthood, an holy nation, a peculiar people; that ye should shew forth the praises of him who hath called you out of darkness into his marvelous light."* (1 Peter 2:9)

> *"But ye shall be named the Priests of the LORD: men shall call you the Ministers of our God: ye shall eat the riches of the Gentiles, and in their glory shall ye boast yourselves."* (Isaiah 61:6)

> *"And he said unto them, When ye pray, say, Our Father which art in heaven, Hallowed be thy name. Thy kingdom come. Thy will be done, as in heaven, so in earth."* (Luke 11:2)

I partner with God

I partner with God as a watchman. God has chosen to use the vehicle of people reaching out to people with His words of warning. He takes no pleasure in punishing the guilty and rebellious. It is an honor for me to sound the alarm, but at the same time, it is also a heavy responsibility if you or I remain silent and allow people to continue on a path that leads to destruction.

> *"Son of man, I have made thee a watchman unto the house of Israel: therefore hear the word at my mouth, and give them warning from me."* (Ezekiel 3:17)

When His Spirit seeks for a man I am available and I make up the hedge. My job is to be available for God. In team sports there are those who are suited up for the game, but may not be starters. Although not starters, they must remain focused, have trained, and be ready for the moment they are called into the fray. So it is with God. I must be ready and responsive when He calls my number and gives me an assignment. I can't sit on the sidelines or question in my heart whether or not I am feeling the leading of the Spirit to act.

> *"And I sought for a man among them, that should make up the hedge, and stand in the gap before me for the land, that I should not destroy it: but I found none."* (Ezekiel 22:30)

I prophesy all that the Lord says for me to declare. I want to be ready to implement what I have heard from God without hesitating for fear of what people will think or that they might persecute me. I admit that there have been times when I remained silent or wanted to wait for more confirmation that what I was sensing was the urging of God. There have also been times when I have attempted to make God's words more palatable by editing them to soften them. I thank God for His patience with me and for causing me to grow in boldness.

> *"Then I said, I will not make mention of him, nor speak any more in his name. But [his word] was in mine heart as a burning fire shut up in my bones, and I was weary with forbearing, and I could not [stay]."* (Jeremiah 20:9)

I work the works of God. I want to do what Jesus did. That is how He taught His disciples to function. He did not laugh at Peter and discount his request to join Him in walking on the water. He said "come," and so invited Peter to go for it. The fact that Jesus would use words like "whosoever" and "whatsoever" when giving instruction on the promises of God means you and I, as believers, are eligible candidates to work the works of God.

> *"Then said they unto him, What shall we do, that we might work the works of God?"* (John 6:28)

> *"Believest thou not that I am in the Father, and the Father in me? The words that I speak unto you I speak not of myself: but the Father that dwelleth in me, he doeth the works. Believe*

me that I [am] in the Father, and the Father in me: or else believe me for the very works' sake. Verily, verily, I say unto you, he that believeth on me, the works that I do shall he do also; and greater [works] than these shall he do; because I go unto my Father. And whatsoever ye shall ask in my name, that will I do, that the Father may be glorified in the Son. If ye shall ask any thing in my name, I will do [it]." (John 14:10-14)

I pray without ceasing and my righteous prayers have power with God. I practice the presence of God and speak with Holy Spirit God through the day. I pray for people and situations as God prompts me to do so and God answers the prayers that He prompts me to pray out. It is His pleasure for us to work in tandem and for me to go about in the confidence of a son of God using my God inspired prayers and actions to extend the rule and authority of the Kingdom of God.

Pray for people and situations as God prompts

"Praying always with all prayer and supplication in the Spirit, and watching thereunto with all perseverance and supplication for all saints." (Ephesians 6:18)

"...pray one for another, that ye may be healed. The effectual fervent prayer of a righteous man availeth much." (James 5:16)

CHAPTER 3
I KNOW AND EXTOL THE
NATURE AND WAYS OF GOD

I don't doubt the Word of God or His nature. The essence of His Character is that He is good, peaceful, true, compassionate, kind, longsuffering, willing, excellent, pure, honorable, virtuous, Divine, venerable, adorable, holy, righteous, perfect, light, spirit, invisible, existential, glorious, splendorous, beautiful, unchanging, ineffable, incomparable, limitless, boundless, omnipresent, worthy, trustworthy, discerning, knowing, omniscient, understanding, humble, great, the head, transcendent, supreme, most high, Alpha and Omega, ancient of days, eternal, immortal, sovereign, majestic, wise, gentle, faithful, merciful, gracious, just, wonderful, benevolent, beneficent, passionate, and loving.

God continues to reveal Himself

I don't doubt the Word of God or His nature. I believe most people have a limited knowledge of God because they may have voluntarily estranged themselves from God, or considered God to be like them, or have not sought His face, or are satisfied with a superficial knowledge of God and lack the thirst to know His nature and ways in a fuller measure.

23

The Bible is full of revelation about the nature and ways of God. As men and women encountered Him He revealed insights into His nature and ways that are captured in scripture. God continues to reveal Himself to me today too as I seek Him and worshipfully love Him. In the process I am amazed and overcome by His love and by a greater realization of who He is.

> *"But let the one who boasts boast about this: that they have the understanding to know me, that I am the LORD, who exercises kindness, justice and righteousness on earth, for in these I delight, declares the LORD.* (Jeremiah 9:24 NIV)

The heart's cry of the apostle Paul was to know God. The man who had special visitations of the resurrected savior and to whom it was granted to perform special miracles because of his calling and fellowship with the Lord, still yearned to know God in a fuller measure. I too have the desire to really know my God.

> *"That I may know him, and the power of his resurrection, and the fellowship of his sufferings, being made conformable unto his death."* (Philippians 3:10)

The Essence of the Character of God

The essence of His Character. Let us begin by examining the essence of the character of God. This examination will proceed word by word. Where some characteristics are very close in meaning they have been grouped together. I don't consider those characteristics to be redundant and unnecessary repetition, but rather to be overlapping, with much in common, yet adding additional insight into the character of God.

Good. God is a good God. Without this realization I would fear drawing close to Him.

> *"For thou, Lord, [art] good, and ready to forgive; and plenteous in mercy unto all them that call upon thee.* (Psalm 86:5)

> *"They shall abundantly utter the memory of thy great goodness, and shall sing of thy righteousness. The LORD [is] gracious, and full of compassion; slow to anger, and of great mercy. The LORD [is] good to all: and his tender mercies [are] over all his works."* (Psalm 145:7-9)

Peaceful. To enter into God's presence is to experience peace. The prophet Isaiah, speaking by God, declared that the coming Messiah would be called the Prince of Peace. The birth of Jesus was heralded by angels with a declaration of peace. I have made peace with God and enjoy His peace in my life.

> *"And the very God of peace sanctify you wholly; and [I pray God] your whole spirit and soul and body be preserved blameless unto the coming of our Lord Jesus Christ."* (1 Thessalonians 5:23)

True. God is reliably true. Because He is true, our faith in Him and His word rests on a firm foundation. Jesus is the true God. All others are liars, pretenders, and part of a deception. Once I was visiting Darjeeling, India and asked directions from a Buddhist monk on the street. Later that evening, he came to my hotel room and asked me to tell him about Jesus. As we sat by the fireplace on a cold night at a high altitude in sight of the snow covered Himalayan Mountains, I gladly took the opportunity to share with him about the true God.

> *"And I saw heaven opened, and behold a white horse; and he that sat upon him [was] called Faithful and True, and in righteousness he doth judge and make war."* (Revelation 19:11)

> *"And the LORD passed by before him, and proclaimed, The LORD, The LORD God, merciful and gracious, longsuffering, and abundant in goodness and truth."* (Exodus 34:6)

"And we know that the Son of God is come, and hath given us an understanding, that we may know him that is true, and we are in him that is true, [even] in his Son Jesus Christ. This is the true God, and eternal life." (1 John 5:20)

Compassionate, kind, and longsuffering. If God were not compassionate, kind, and longsuffering mankind would not continue to exist on earth. I know I have failed many times and would have a place reserved in hell, but for the fact that my God is compassionate, kind, and longsuffering toward me.

"But thou, O Lord, [art] a God full of compassion, and gracious, longsuffering, and plenteous in mercy and truth." (Psalm 86:15)

Willing. As high as God is above mankind, He is willing to relate to man, demonstrate His love, and manifest His power over all the problems that confront us. I am so glad that God was willing to show me mercy, change my life, and give me the honor of using His name.

"And, behold, there came a leper and worshipped him, saying, Lord, if thou wilt, thou canst make me clean. And Jesus put forth [his] hand, and touched him, saying, I will; be thou clean. And immediately his leprosy was cleansed." (Matthew 8:2-3)

"And whatsoever ye shall ask in my name, that will I do, that the Father may be glorified in the Son. If ye shall ask any thing in my name, I will do [it]." (John 14:13-14)

Excellent. God is not common or mediocre. He is excellent in name and deeds. I want to be like Him and live a life of excellence by His power.

"O LORD our Lord, how excellent [is] thy name in all the earth!" (Psalm 8:9)

26

Pure. God is not only pure, but He cannot be contaminated or defiled by me and my uncleanliness. When Jesus took my sins and the sins of the world on Himself that did not damn Him. He paid the price and God the Father restored Him to the same glory and purity He knew with the Father from eons past. When I approach Him on His terms He purifies me with His blood and His word so that I can fellowship with Him.

> *"And every man that hath this hope in him purifieth himself, even as he is pure."* (1 John 3:3)

Honorable. Honoring God in my worship by affirming that He is honorable is essential to knowing Him.

> *"Glory and honour [are] in his presence; strength and gladness [are] in his place."* (1 Chronicles 16:27)

> *"And every creature which is in heaven, and on the earth, and under the earth, and such as are in the sea, and all that are in them, heard I saying, Blessing, and honour, and glory, and power, [be] unto him that sitteth upon the throne, and unto the Lamb for ever and ever."* (Revelation 5:13)

> *"Let us be glad and rejoice, and give honour to him: for the marriage of the Lamb is come, and his wife hath made herself ready."* (Revelation 19:7)

Virtuous. In contemplating the virtue of God I am changed more and more into that same likeness. His virtue is something that I draw upon, because I have no virtue in myself apart from Him.

> *"And Jesus said, Somebody hath touched me: for I perceive that virtue is gone out of me."* (Luke 8:46)

Divine, venerable and adorable. Only God is divine and to be venerated and adored. However, it pleases Him to place His nature in me and

live in me that I may approach Him, through the work of Christ, so that
I may worship Him.

> *"According as his divine power hath given unto us all things
> that [pertain] unto life and godliness, through the knowledge
> of him that hath called us to glory and virtue."* (2 Peter 1:3)

Holy, righteous, and perfect. God's nature is so high above my nature
that I am utterly humbled in His presence knowing my unworthiness
apart from His gift in transforming me. He makes me holy, bestows His
righteousness upon me, and perfects me for Himself.

> *"And ye shall be holy unto me: for I the LORD [am] holy, and
> have severed you from [other] people, that ye should be mine."*
> (Leviticus 20:26)

> *"[As for] God, his way [is] perfect: the word of the LORD is
> tried: he [is] a buckler to all those that trust in him."* (Psalm
> 18:30)

> *"The LORD [is] righteous in all his ways, and holy in all his
> works."* (Psalm 145:17)

> *"For thus saith the high and lofty One that inhabiteth eter-
> nity, whose name [is] Holy; I dwell in the high and holy
> [place], with him also [that is] of a contrite and humble spirit,
> to revive the spirit of the humble, and to revive the heart of
> the contrite ones."* (Isaiah 57:15)

> *"Be ye therefore perfect, even as your Father which is in heaven
> is perfect."* (Matthew 5:48)

Light, spirit, and invisible. I am a flesh and blood person and live in
the dimension of the physical universe. But God has also given me a
spirit that I might worship Him in spirit.

> *"This then is the message which we have heard of him, and
> declare unto you, that God is light, and in him is no darkness
> at all."* (1 John 1:5)

"Now unto the King eternal, immortal, invisible, the only wise God, [be] honour and glory for ever and ever. Amen." (1 Timothy 1:17)

"God [is] a Spirit: and they that worship him must worship [him] in spirit and in truth." (John 4:14)

"By faith he forsook Egypt, not fearing the wrath of the king: for he endured, as seeing him who is invisible." (Hebrews 11:27)

"The wind bloweth where it listeth, and thou hearest the sound thereof, but canst not tell whence it cometh, and whither it goeth: so is every one that is born of the Spirit." (John 3:8)

Existential. God is. There never was and never will be a time when that truth is not so. Early in my introduction to Italy, while driving around Tuscany, I saw the simple message in Italian scrawled on bridges and walls "God is." I recognize that He is and that I am in need of Him.

"And God said unto Moses, I AM THAT I AM: and he said, Thus shalt thou say unto the children of Israel, I AM hath sent me unto you." (Exodus 3:14)

"John to the seven churches which are in Asia: Grace [be] unto you, and peace, from him which is, and which was, and which is to come; and from the seven Spirits which are before his throne." Revelation 1:4)

Glorious, splendorous, and beautiful. The creator of beautiful things is Himself the fountain from which beauty flows. He is the epitome of splendor, glory, and beauty. As much as I enjoy the beauty of the things He has created, my deepest desire is to be in His presence and look on Him in all of His glory and splendor.

"One [thing] have I desired of the LORD, that will I seek after; that I may dwell in the house of the LORD all the days

of my life, to behold the beauty of the LORD, and to enquire in his temple." (Psalm 27:4)

"I [am] the LORD: that [is] my name: and my glory will I not give to another, neither my praise to graven images." (Isaiah 42:8)

Unchanging. I can be fickle, moody, and given to attempting makeovers and resolutions. God is rock solid unchangeable and has bound Himself by His own words concerning me so that I am not destroyed.

"For I [am] the LORD, I change not; therefore ye sons of Jacob are not consumed." (Malachi 3:6)

Ineffable and incomparable. Words and comparisons fail to do justice to who God is and how high He is above me and my ways.

"Who [is] like unto thee, O LORD, among the gods? who [is] like thee, glorious in holiness, fearful [in] praises, doing wonders?" (Exodus 15:11)

Limitless, boundless, and omnipresent. Man is finite. Man's greatest space triumph only reveals how limited is our domain. I serve a God who knows no limits. The fact that He can be everywhere at the same time means that He has the capacity to be a doting father to me and to all others on a personal level, at the same time.

"Whither shall I go from thy spirit? Or whither shall I flee from thy presence? If I ascend up into heaven, thou [art] there: if I make my bed in hell, behold, thou [art there]. [If] I take the wings of the morning, [and] dwell in the uttermost parts of the sea; even there shall thy hand lead me, and thy right hand shall hold me." (Psalm 139:7-10)

"But who is able to build him an house, seeing the heaven and heaven of heavens cannot contain him? Who [am] I then, that I should build him an house, save only to burn sacrifice before him?" (2 Chronicles 2:6)

Worthy and trustworthy. God is in a class by Himself. He alone is worthy of my praise and worship. I place full trust in Him and His word.

> *"And they sung a new song, saying, Thou art worthy to take the book, and to open the seals thereof: for thou wast slain, and hast redeemed us to God by thy blood out of every kindred, and tongue, and people, and nation."* (Revelation 5:9)

> *"For therefore we both labour and suffer reproach, because we trust in the living God, who is the Saviour of all men, specially of those that believe."* (1Timothy 4:10)

Discerning, knowing, omniscient, and understanding. All the books in the world and the rapidity with which books of human knowledge become outdated serve to show how little we know or understand. When I was part of the faculty at a major university I was proud of my first scholarly book. I lived in a world of "publish or perish." As cutting edge as I and my colleagues thought our work was, it all became quickly outdated and unmarketable. My field of the social sciences was heavy with theory, but light on acknowledged hard and fast laws. But there is one who knows all things great and small, from the past and to the future, and from whom nothing can be hid.

> *"[To the chief Musician, A Psalm of David.] O LORD, thou hast searched me, and known [me]. Thou knowest my downsitting and mine uprising, thou understandest my thought afar off. Thou compassest my path and my lying down, and art acquainted [with] all my ways. For [there is] not a word in my tongue, [but], lo, O LORD, thou knowest it altogether."* (Psalm 139:1-4)

> *"Great [is] our Lord, and of great power: his understanding [is] infinite."* (Psalm 147:5)

Humble. Men value traits of self-confidence, assertiveness, and leaders who step forward and take command. God, in His greatness, nevertheless modeled for man a spirit of humility. When I am tempted to be arrogant or lapse into talking down to others, I have to repent and remember the way of humility shown by Jesus.

> *"Let this mind be in you, which was also in Christ Jesus: who, being in the form of God, thought it not robbery to be equal with God: but made himself of no reputation, and took upon him the form of a servant, and was made in the likeness of men: and being found in fashion as a man, he humbled himself, and became obedient unto death, even the death of the cross. Wherefore God also hath highly exalted him, and given him a name which is above every name: that at the name of Jesus every knee should bow, of [things] in heaven, and [things] in earth, and [things] under the earth; and [that] every tongue should confess that Jesus Christ [is] Lord, to the glory of God the Father.* (Philippians 2:5-11)

> *"Take my yoke upon you, and learn of me; for I am meek and lowly in heart: and ye shall find rest unto your souls."* (Matthew 11:29)

Great, the head, transcendent, supreme, and most high. There are not enough superlatives to describe God. To know Him in His greatness is to hold Him in awesome reverence and worship.

> *"For thou [art] great, and doest wondrous things: thou [art] God alone."* (Psalm 86:10)

> *"That [men] may know that thou, whose name alone [is] JEHOVAH, [art] the most high over all the earth." Psalm 83:18)*

> *"Thine, O LORD, [is] the greatness, and the power, and the glory, and the victory, and the majesty: for all [that is] in the heaven and in the earth [is thine]; thine [is] the kingdom, O LORD, and thou art exalted as head above all."* (1 Chronicles 29:11)

Alpha and Omega, ancient of days, eternal, and immortal. God is the sum of all things. He alone exists from the everlasting past to the everlasting future. It is His will for me to draw near to Him and to know this aspect of His nature.

> *"The eternal God [is thy] refuge, and underneath [are] the everlasting arms: and he shall thrust out the enemy from before thee; and shall say, Destroy [them]."* (Deuteronomy 33:27)

> *"Now unto the King eternal, immortal, invisible, the only wise God, [be] honour and glory for ever and ever. Amen."* (1 Timothy 1:17)

> *"And he said unto me, It is done. I am Alpha and Omega, the beginning and the end. I will give unto him that is athirst of the fountain of the water of life freely."* (Revelation 21:6)

Sovereign and majestic. The majesty and dominion of God is not a myth from the imagination of man. I have traveled the world and observed the things and ideas men worship. I also know that there are rebellious spirits that demonstrate power that convinces some men to accept their lies. This I know, God is real and rules over all. There is the historical record of those who walked with Jesus and there is my own experience with God that confirms their testimony and His word.

> *"For we have not followed cunningly devised fables, when we made known unto you the power and coming of our Lord Jesus Christ, but were eyewitnesses of his majesty. For he received from God the Father honour and glory, when there came such a voice to him from the excellent glory, This is my beloved Son, in whom I am well pleased."* (2 Peter 1:16-17)

Wise. God is all wisdom and He gives wisdom to those seek Him for it. I have sought for His wisdom and He has not disappointed me.

> *"Now unto the King eternal, immortal, invisible, the only wise God, [be] honour and glory for ever and ever. Amen."* (1 Timothy 1:17)

Gentle. God is gentle in His ways and will not force men to accept His gifts. He leads His sheep gently and does not drive them. I have chosen to follow my gentle savior.

> *"But the wisdom that is from above is first pure, then peaceable, gentle, [and] easy to be intreated, full of mercy and good fruits, without partiality, and without hypocrisy."* (James 3:17)

Faithful. God is forever faithful and reliable in His ways and in His promises to me. When I stand in faith I often remind myself that God is faithful and I speak that truth out loud.

> *"And I saw heaven opened, and behold a white horse; and he that sat upon him [was] called Faithful and True, and in righteousness he doth judge and make war."* (Revelation 19:11)

Merciful and gracious. Without the grace and mercy of God, there would be no hope for me to avoid hell. He has instead called me to be with Him forever. I am in awe of His great grace and mercy toward me.

> *"And the LORD descended in the cloud, and stood with him there, and proclaimed the name of the LORD. And the LORD passed by before him, and proclaimed, The LORD, The LORD God, merciful and gracious, longsuffering, and abundant in goodness and truth, keeping mercy for thousands, forgiving iniquity and transgression and sin, and that will by no means clear [the guilty]; visiting the iniquity of the fathers upon the children, and upon the children's children, unto the third and to the fourth [generation]."* (Exodus 34:5-7)

> *"But the God of all grace, who hath called us unto his eternal glory by Christ Jesus, after that ye have suffered a while, make you perfect, stablish, strengthen, settle [you]."* (1 Peter 5:10)

Just. God is just and fair, even at His own expense to pay the penalty that I deserved. What He did for me He also did for the whole world. However, those who reject Him must justly pay the penalty for their own sins and rebellion.

> *"Can someone who hates justice govern? Will you condemn the just and mighty One?"* (Job 34:17 NIV)

> *"Behold, the days come, saith the LORD, that I will raise unto David a righteous Branch, and a King shall reign and prosper, and shall execute judgment and justice in the earth."* (Jeremiah 23:5)

Wonderful. God not only does wonders, but who He is and His ways causes me to stop in wonder.

> *"For unto us a child is born, unto us a son is given: and the government shall be upon his shoulder: and his name shall be called Wonderful, Counsellor, The mighty God, The everlasting Father, The Prince of Peace. Of the increase of [his] government and peace [there shall be] no end, upon the throne of David, and upon his kingdom, to order it, and to establish it with judgment and with justice from henceforth even for ever. The zeal of the LORD of hosts will perform this."* (Isaiah 9:6-7)

Benevolent and beneficent. God is extremely generous and overflowing in blessings toward me.

> *"Bless the LORD, O my soul, and forget not all his benefits."* (Psalm 103:2)

> *"Blessed [be] the Lord, [who] daily loadeth us [with benefits, even] the God of our salvation. Selah."* (Psalm 68:19)

Passionate and loving. The story of God's love for us and of His passionate pursuit of us is the greatest story ever told. His passionate love melted my heart.

"He that loveth not knoweth not God; for God is love. In this was manifested the love of God toward us, because that God sent his only begotten Son into the world, that we might live through him. Herein is love, not that we loved God, but that he loved us, and sent his Son [to be] the propitiation for our sins." (1 John 4:8-10)

"Let him kiss me with the kisses of his mouth: for thy love [is] better than wine. Because of the savour of thy good ointments thy name [is as] ointment poured forth, therefore do the virgins love thee. Draw me, we will run after thee: the king hath brought me into his chambers: we will be glad and rejoice in thee, we will remember thy love more than wine: the upright love thee." (Song of Solomon 1:2-4)

God's Nature in His Works

His nature in His works is marvelous, miraculous, mighty, almighty, omnipotent, awesome, creative, life-giving, powerful, redeeming, saving, all conquering, victorious, planning, and working.

Marvelous. God's deeds make men take note in wonderment. I just stand back and smile with joyous praise when God does something marvelous in my life.

"Praise be to the LORD God, the God of Israel, who alone does marvelous deeds." (Psalm 72:18 NIV)

"But the men marvelled, saying, What manner of man is this, that even the winds and the sea obey him!" (Matthew 8:27)

Miraculous. God not only is orderly and sets the laws of the physical universe, but he is able to supersede them to show his power. I expect the miraculous from God.

"You are the God who performs miracles; you display your power among the peoples." (Psalm 77:14 NIV)

Mighty, almighty, and omnipotent. The power of God is unlimited. There is nothing that He cannot do. I ask big things of God because nothing is too hard for Him.

Ask big things of God

"And when Abram was ninety years old and nine, the LORD appeared to Abram, and said unto him, I [am] the Almighty God; walk before me, and be thou perfect." (Genesis 17:1)

"And I heard as it were the voice of a great multitude, and as the voice of many waters, and as the voice of mighty thunderings, saying, Alleluia: for the Lord God omnipotent reigneth." (Revelation 19:6)

Awesome. The demonstration of God's power and the revelation of His greatness leaves me speechless in awestruck wonder.

"Let all the earth fear the LORD: let all the inhabitants of the world stand in awe of him." (Psalm 33:8)

"Then I said: LORD, the God of heaven, the great and awesome God, who keeps his covenant of love with those who love him and keep his commandments." (Nehemiah 1:5 NIV)

"I prayed to the LORD my God and confessed: Lord, the great and awesome God, who keeps his covenant of love with those who love him and keep his commandments." (Daniel 9:4 NIV)

Creative and life-giving. There was nothing before God, who always was, and nothing that exists came into being without Him. Scientists have tried in vain to create life or find evidence of life on another planet. All life is by God. The devil is a destroyer and murderer. I choose the life-giving creator God.

"Thou art worthy, O Lord, to receive glory and honour and power: for thou hast created all things, and for thy pleasure they are and were created." (Revelation 4:11)

Powerful. The power of God is demonstrated by acts no other person or god can even begin to attain to or think about. Yet, because I belong to Him, I can walk in His power.

"Be thou exalted, LORD, in thine own strength: [so] will we sing and praise thy power." (Psalm 21:13)

"Who sent his glorious arm of power to be at Moses' right hand, who divided the waters before them, to gain for himself everlasting renown." (Isaiah 63:12 NIV)

Redeeming and saving. God is the only one that can save men from calamity or indeed is able to save souls. I am so glad that He saved me and sent His Son to save the world.

"[As for] our redeemer, the LORD of hosts [is] his name, the Holy One of Israel." (Isaiah 47:4)

"Thus saith the LORD, thy Redeemer, the Holy One of Israel; I [am] the LORD thy God which teacheth thee to profit, which leadeth thee by the way [that] thou shouldest go." (Isaiah 48:17)

"Though Noah, Daniel, and Job, [were] in it, [as] I live, saith the Lord GOD, they shall deliver neither son nor daughter; they shall [but] deliver their own souls by their righteousness." (Ezekiel 14:20)

All conquering and victorious. Men draw the wrong conclusion from the longsuffering of God. He has never lost a battle. Not long ago my wife and I faced a battle over income taxes to the federal and state governments. It was unjust. Added to it were penalties and interest that made for a great sum of money, more than the median American gross annual household income. Finally, we received a letter informing us that, in less than a week, our home would be auctioned off to cover this unjust tax debt. We did not abandon our faith in the God of victory and would proclaim out loud that He gives us the victory. That week it was all turned around. First the federal government and then the District of Columbia government acknowledged our position. The large tax bills were not only cancelled, but we were sent substantial tax refunds making for a large amount when figuring the difference between what had been billed us and what was eventually given to us. We celebrated victory! God has also given us other victories of a similar nature that were even larger.

> *"But thanks [be] to God, which giveth us the victory through our Lord Jesus Christ."* (1 Corinthians 15:57)

Planning. It is God's delight to plan and to implement His plans. Creationists can clearly point to the hand of a master designer in all aspects of nature as evidence of God. Most important to me, I know that God has good plans for my life.

> *"For I know the plans I have for you, declares the LORD, plans to prosper you and not to harm you, plans to give you hope and a future."* (Jeremiah 29:11 NIV)

Working. God's works cannot be duplicated apart from Him. When I recall the works God has done it increases my faith for the current battle. In addition, when I align myself with His will and word, I can work the works of God by His Spirit.

> *"They kept not the covenant of God, and refused to walk in his law; and forgat his works, and his wonders that he had shewed them. Marvelous things did he in the sight of their fathers, in the land of Egypt, [in] the field of Zoan."* (Psalm 78:10-12)

"Then said they unto him, What shall we do, that we might work the works of God?" (John 6:28)

God's Nature in His Emotional Feelings

His nature in His emotional feeling is joyous, jealous, furious, tender, and suffering.

Joyous. God is a God of joy and it is His pleasure that I should enter into His joy. I want more of the joy found in His presence.

"Thou wilt shew me the path of life: in thy presence [is] fulness of joy; at thy right hand [there are] pleasures for evermore." (Psalm 16:11)

Jealous and furious. Like a jealous spouse, God takes vengeance on those that would attack His own. He also will not suffer being rejected for things that are not God. Once I went to the simple home of a sick elderly woman in Africa, along with a missionary and a believing interpreter. When we noticed that she had charms and other items of the occult in her home we asked her to get rid of them and rely only on God. She initially refused, but when I explained that God is like a jealous spouse, she understood and willingly gave those things to us for burning. She also perked up as evidence of healing taking place in her body from our unhindered prayers for her.

"Thou shalt have no other gods before me. Thou shalt not make unto thee any graven image, or any likeness [of any thing] that [is] in heaven above, or that [is] in the earth beneath, or that [is] in the water under the earth: Thou shalt not bow down thyself to them, nor serve them: for I the LORD thy God [am] a jealous God, visiting the iniquity of the fathers upon the children unto the third and fourth [generation] of them that hate me." (Exodus 20:3-5)

"God [is] jealous, and the LORD revengeth; the LORD revengeth, and [is] furious; the LORD will take vengeance

on his adversaries, and he reserveth [wrath] for his enemies."
(Nahum 1:2)

"For the LORD thy God [is] a consuming fire, [even] a jealous God." (Deuteronomy 4:24)

Tender. God not only sent His son into the world as a tender baby, but He is tender and is hurt when we slight Him. Part of my relationship with God is for me to be sensitive to how my words and ways can hurt Him so that I limit that behavior. In the same manner, when I fail to make time for God, it is like a rejection of His love that hurts the one I love.

"For he shall grow up before him as a tender plant, and as a root out of a dry ground: he hath no form nor comeliness; and when we shall see him, [there is] no beauty that we should desire him." (Isaiah 53:2)

Suffering. It is a measure of the love of God that He allowed Himself to suffer for me and for the world.

"But he [was] wounded for our transgressions, [he was] bruised for our iniquities: the chastisement of our peace [was] upon him; and with his stripes we are healed." (Isaiah 53:5)

"And being in an agony he prayed more earnestly: and his sweat was as it were great drops of blood falling down to the ground." (Luke 22:44)

God's Nature as Revealed in His Functions

His nature in His functions is judging, governing, ruling, avenging, prophetic, interceding, reconciling, high priest, savior, Lamb of God, redeemer, Christ, Messiah, author and finisher of our faith.

Judging. God judges to reward, to avenge, or to punish. I want to live so as to be worthy of His rewards. On one occasion as I stood in the famous baptistery of Florence, Italy, next to the cathedral Santa Maria del Fiore, with its beautiful mosaics on themes from the Bible, I listened as an art historian told a group that the hands of the central figure, Jesus Christ, had an error such that the thumb on one hand was pointed the wrong way. He was dead wrong. My daughter has a degree in art history and I am a lover of art, but I also know the Bible. What the artists depicted was Jesus sitting in judgment with one hand welcoming believers into the rewards of His kingdom while the other hand was giving the back of His hand in rejection to others as if to say "Depart from me, I never knew you." Thus the original artists well understood the notion that Jesus Christ judges both to reward and to punish as appropriate.

> *"And therefore will the LORD wait, that he may be gracious unto you, and therefore will he be exalted, that he may have mercy upon you: for the LORD [is] a God of judgment: blessed [are] all they that wait for him."* (Isaiah 30:18)

Governing and ruling. God rules in heaven above and on earth. His righteous rule will be established over the earth when rebellious spirits and unrepentant, rebellious men are ultimately quarantined in hell for eternity.

> *"For unto us a child is born, unto us a son is given: and the government shall be upon his shoulder: and his name shall be called Wonderful, Counsellor, The mighty God, The everlasting Father, The Prince of Peace. Of the increase of [his] government and peace [there shall be] no end, upon the throne of David, and upon his kingdom, to order it, and to establish it with judgment and with justice from henceforth even for ever. The zeal of the LORD of hosts will perform this."* (Isaiah 9:6-7)

Avenging. Vengeance is a prerogative of God. I am what is known as a warm reactive. Even if I manage to make my outside look cool when provoked, inside my blood pressure spikes. I want to avoid fits of temper and giving in to the desire to take vengeance myself.

> *"Dearly beloved, avenge not yourselves, but [rather] give place unto wrath: for it is written, Vengeance [is] mine; I will repay, saith the Lord."* (Romans 12:19)

> *"O LORD God, to whom vengeance belongeth; O God, to whom vengeance belongeth, shew thyself."* (Psalm 94:1)

Prophetic. Because God cannot lie, what He says happens, though there may be a time-lag due to His mercy. God shared with the prophets the mystery of His redeemer and of the age of the church of Jesus. When I obediently speak God's words concerning Jesus I flow in the spirit of prophesy.

> *"And I fell at his feet to worship him. And he said unto me, See [thou do it] not: I am thy fellowservant, and of thy brethren that have the testimony of Jesus: worship God: for the testimony of Jesus is the spirit of prophecy."* (Revelation 19:10)

Interceding. God is a righteous judge, but to avoid total destruction of rebellious and sinful humankind, He gave the ministry of intercession to God the Son and to Holy Spirit God. God is also looking for me and other believers to partner with Him in the ministry of intercession.

> *"And he saw that [there was] no man, and wondered that [there was] no intercessor: therefore his arm brought salvation unto him; and his righteousness, it sustained him."* (Isaiah 59:16)

"And he that searcheth the hearts knoweth what [is] the mind of the Spirit, because he maketh intercession for the saints according to [the will of] God."

Reconciling, high priest, savior, Lamb of God, redeemer, Christ, and Messiah. Without God Himself performing the functions listed above toward and for mankind, as part of His nature, there would be no hope for mankind, but instead a permanent separation from God. My salvation is secured by the work of God. Nothing I can do, apart from His grace, can save me.

"And the angel said unto them, Fear not: for, behold, I bring you good tidings of great joy, which shall be to all people. For unto you is born this day in the city of David a Saviour, which is Christ the Lord." (Luke 2:10-11)

"The Spirit of the Lord GOD [is] upon me; because the LORD hath anointed me to preach good tidings unto the meek; he hath sent me to bind up the brokenhearted, to proclaim liberty to the captives, and the opening of the prison to [them that are] bound." (Isaiah 61:1)

"Then came the Jews round about him, and said unto him, How long dost thou make us to doubt? If thou be the Christ, tell us plainly. Jesus answered them, I told you, and ye believed not: the works that I do in my Father's name, they bear witness of me." (John 10:24-25)

"Wherefore, holy brethren, partakers of the heavenly calling, consider the Apostle and High Priest of our profession, Christ Jesus." (Hebrews 3:1)

"Seeing then that we have a great high priest, that is passed into the heavens, Jesus the Son of God, let us hold fast [our] profession. For we have not an high priest which cannot be touched with the feeling of our infirmities; but was in all points tempted like as [we are, yet] without sin. Let us therefore come boldly unto the throne of grace, that we may obtain mercy, and find grace to help in time of need." (Hebrews 4:14-16)

"The next day John seeth Jesus coming unto him, and saith, Behold the Lamb of God, which taketh away the sin of the world." (John 1:29)

Author and finisher of our faith. Before man was ever created, God, in His omniscience, foresaw the need for a savior, and the Godhead agreed on the plan for the salvation of this race of people that would require something new from God—great sacrifice, pain, and shame. But, foreseeing the joy that would come afterward, the great adventure began.

> *"Looking unto Jesus the author and finisher of [our] faith; who for the joy that was set before him endured the cross, despising the shame, and is set down at the right hand of the throne of God."* (Hebrews 12:2)

God's Nature Seen in His Relationships

His nature in His relations is Lord, Master, Father, bridegroom, kinsman-redeemer, brother, Emmanuel, approachable, friendly, caring, nurturing, comforting, healing, beckoning, longsuffering, selfless, forgiving, counseling, sharing, serving, advocating, and mediating.

Lord and Master. God is my Lord and Master, but He allows me to decide whether I will draw near in that relationship or rebel. However, no rebellion can change His nature in this matter. Every knee will bow and every tongue confess His lordship.

> *"Ye call me Master and Lord: and ye say well; for [so] I am."* (John 13:13)

> *"And, behold, one came and said unto him, Good Master, what good thing shall I do, that I may have eternal life?"* (Matthew 19:16)

> *"For it is written, [As] I live, saith the Lord, every knee shall bow to me, and every tongue shall confess to God."* (Romans 14:11)

Father. God is my Father and He is also the Father of an innumerable family. He has the ability to make each of His children feel special in their relationship with Him.

"For as many as are led by the Spirit of God, they are the sons of God. For ye have not received the spirit of bondage again to fear; but ye have received the Spirit of adoption, whereby we cry, Abba, Father. The Spirit itself beareth witness with our spirit, that we are the children of God And if children, then heirs; heirs of God, and joint-heirs with Christ; if so be that we suffer with [him], that we may be also glorified together." (Romans 8:14-17)

Bridegroom. God chose the metaphor of bridegroom to help us understand that He has betrothed Himself to us and will one day celebrate His marriage to us with all of the affection and unity that entails. I rejoice in that I have been chosen by God to be forever bound together with Him.

"And Jesus said unto them, Can the children of the bride-chamber fast, while the bridegroom is with them? As long as they have the bridegroom with them, they cannot fast. But the days will come, when the bridegroom shall be taken away from them, and then shall they fast in those days." (Mark 2:19-20)

Kinsman-redeemer. God became man and entered the earth where He partook of a flesh and blood existence through the portal of the womb of the Virgin Mary. He had to have a human body capable of dying so that it could be put to death as a sacrifice for the sins of the world. No other man could do it because all men were stained by the sin nature inherited from Adam. No angel could do it because they are immortal and of a different type of being. Besides, God will not share His glory with another. He filled this function of kinsman redeemer Himself, allowing Himself to be humbled in the process. Such love draws me to Him and inspires worship.

"But we see Jesus, who was made a little lower than the angels for the suffering of death, crowned with glory and honour; that he by the grace of God should taste death for every man." (Hebrews 2:9)

Brother. God is not only our Father, but through God the Son He has become our elder brother. God has made me part of His family and there is room for many others to enjoy that experience and honor.

> *"For whosoever shall do the will of my Father which is in heaven, the same is my brother, and sister, and mother."* (Matthew 12:50)

> *"For whom he did foreknow, he also did predestinate [to be] conformed to the image of his Son, that he might be the first-born among many brethren."* (Romans 8:29)

God is with us

Emmanuel. God is with us, is for us, and He and loves us. We, the human race, are His baby, His special project. This is the God that came down from heaven in human form, but not yet human born, to have a meal with His friend Abraham. This is the God who lived on a day-to-day basis for several years with close disciples. During that time He walked with them from town to town making Himself available to those in need or who were awaiting the Messiah, as He declared that the Kingdom of God had come to them. He hugged and blessed children and made sure that they had access to Him. He frequented the home of Mary, Martha, and Lazarus just to be with them as a friend. In the protocol of some of the royalty of this world, common people are not allowed to touch royals. But Jesus, our Emmanuel, allowed crowds to press in on Him grasping and touching Him. He also touched and healed a leper when no one else would touch a leprous person. He told His followers that He had to go away from them (back to heaven), but would prepare a place for them, and us, where we could live with Him forever. He also promised that He would send another just like Himself, God the Holy Spirit, to live in each of us that believe on Him as God the Son. Then, after giving His life to make an acceptable payment for the sins of the world, He rose again and promised, before He ascended back to heaven, that He would always be with us. He will come again and rule the earth from a literal throne where all nationalities and ethnic groups will come to Him and see Him.

> *"Therefore the Lord himself shall give you a sign; Behold, a virgin shall conceive, and bear a son, and shall call his name Immanuel."* (Isaiah 7:14)

> *"Behold, a virgin shall be with child, and shall bring forth a son, and they shall call his name Emmanuel, which being interpreted is, God with us."* (Matthew 1:23)

> *"And the LORD appeared unto him in the plains of Mamre: and he sat in the tent door in the heat of the day; and he lift up his eyes and looked, and, lo, three men stood by him: and when he saw [them], he ran to meet them from the tent door, and bowed himself toward the ground." Genesis 18:1-2)*

> *"Then I was by him, [as] one brought up [with him]: and I was daily [his] delight, rejoicing always before him; Rejoicing in the habitable part of his earth; and my delights [were] with the sons of men."* (Proverbs 8:30-31)

> *"Come unto me, all [ye] that labour and are heavy laden, and I will give you rest."* (Matthew 11:28)

> *"And I will pray the Father, and he shall give you another Comforter, that he may abide with you for ever."* (John 14:16)

Approachable and friendly. God has made Himself available to mankind. I am invited to be in close relationship and fellowship with Him.

> *"And I heard a great voice out of heaven saying, Behold, the tabernacle of God [is] with men, and he will dwell with them, and they shall be his people, and God himself shall be with them, [and be] their God."* (Revelation 21:3)

Caring, nurturing, comforting, and healing. God cares for me, nurtures and comforts me, and is the source of my healing.

> *"Casting all your care upon him; for he careth for you."* (1 Peter 5:7)

> *"Blessed [be] God, even the Father of our Lord Jesus Christ, the Father of mercies, and the God of all comfort; who comforteth us in all our tribulation, that we may be able to comfort them which are in any trouble, by the comfort wherewith we ourselves are comforted of God."* (2 Corinthians 1:3-4)

> *"But unto you that fear my name shall the Sun of righteousness arise with healing in his wings; and ye shall go forth, and grow up as calves of the stall."* (Malachi 4:2)

Beckoning. God beckons me to come and be in an intimate relationship of fellowship with Him. I would be a fool to resist or turn away. I also want to persuade others to respond to His call.

> *"And the Spirit and the bride say, Come. And let him that heareth say, Come. And let him that is athirst come. And whosoever will, let him take the water of life freely."* (Revelation 22:17)

> *"In the last day, that great [day] of the feast, Jesus stood and cried, saying, If any man thirst, let him come unto me, and drink. He that believeth on me, as the scripture hath said, out of his belly shall flow rivers of living water. (But this spake he of the Spirit, which they that believe on him should receive: for the Holy Ghost was not yet [given]; because that Jesus was not yet glorified.) Many of the people therefore, when they heard this saying, said, Of a truth this is the Prophet. Others said, This is the Christ. But some said, Shall Christ come out of Galilee?"* (John 7:37-41)

Longsuffering. Thanks to God's nature of being longsuffering in His relationship with me, coupled with his mercy and forgiveness, I have the hope of fellowshipping with Him as did Moses.

> *"And the LORD descended in the cloud, and stood with him there, and proclaimed the name of the LORD. And the LORD passed by before him, and proclaimed, The LORD, The LORD God, merciful and gracious, longsuffering, and abundant in goodness and truth, Keeping mercy for thousands, forgiving iniquity and transgression and sin, and that will by no means clear [the guilty]; visiting the iniquity of the fathers upon the children, and upon the children's children, unto the third and to the fourth [generation]."* (Exodus 34:5-7)

Selfless. The love of God toward me was selfless in that He not only gave His life for me, but set aside His glory, and gave Himself up to torture, mocking, humiliation, and having my sins and the sins of the world poured out on His holy self.

> *"Greater love hath no man than this, that a man lay down his life for his friends."* (John 15:13)

Forgiving. The forgiving nature of God toward sinful, but repentant men enables me to be in a relationship of fellowship with Him when I am sorry for my failures and turn to Him.

> *"Thou answeredst them, O LORD our God: thou wast a God that forgavest them, though thou tookest vengeance of their inventions."* (Psalm 99:8)

> *"Bless the LORD, O my soul, and forget not all his benefits: Who forgiveth all thine iniquities; who healeth all thy diseases."* (Psalm 103:2-3)

Counseling. God delights in me seeking His counsel rather than my own way or the opinions and counsel of the ungodly.

"And the spirit of the LORD shall rest upon him, the spirit of wisdom and understanding, the spirit of counsel and might, the spirit of knowledge and of the fear of the LORD." (Isaiah 11:2)

Sharing. God has all things, yet is pleased to allow me and as many as love Him to share in the inheritance of the risen savior Jesus Christ.

"For ye have not received the spirit of bondage again to fear; but ye have received the Spirit of adoption, whereby we cry, Abba, Father. The Spirit itself beareth witness with our spirit, that we are the children of God: and if children, then heirs; heirs of God, and joint-heirs with Christ; if so be that we suffer with [him], that we may be also glorified together." (John 8:15-17)

Serving. The nature of God has been to model for His children how they should live as when Jesus, knowing He came from God and was an integral part of the Godhead, served His disciples by washing their feet. When I serve I am being like Jesus.

"For whether [is] greater, he that sitteth at meat, or he that serveth? [is] not he that sitteth at meat? But I am among you as he that serveth." (Luke 22:27)

Advocating. God the Son advocates for me with His obedient life and blood before the Father.

"My little children, these things write I unto you, that ye sin not. And if any man sin, we have an advocate with the Father, Jesus Christ the righteous." (1 John 2:1)

Mediating. As both God and man, Jesus is the bridge that redeems me and brings me into fellowship with God.

"For [there is] one God, and one mediator between God and men, the man Christ Jesus." (1 Timothy 2:5)

"How much more shall the blood of Christ, who through the eternal Spirit offered himself without spot to God, purge your conscience from dead works to serve the living God? And for this cause he is the mediator of the new testament, that by means of death, for the redemption of the transgressions [that were] under the first testament, they which are called might receive the promise of eternal inheritance." (Hebrews 9:14-15)

God's Nature Seen in His Assistance to and Development of Man

His nature in His assistance to and development of man is covenanting, leading, guiding, shepherding, correcting, chastening, reproving, consuming fire, directing, warring, liberating, delivering, saving, sheltering, protecting, shielding, keeping, purifying, refining, pruning, transforming, regenerating, enlightening, teaching, revealing, warning, pleading, trying, searching, renewing, restoring, sanctifying, perfecting, anointing, strengthening, befriending, satisfying, rewarding, promoting, exalting, favoring, prospering, blessing, and bountiful.

Covenanting. It is God's nature to bind Himself with covenants for the saving and restoration of me and all who willingly come under that covenant.

> *"And he said, LORD God of Israel, [there is] no God like thee, in heaven above, or on earth beneath, who keepest covenant and mercy with thy servants that walk before thee with all their heart."* (1 Kings 8:23)

Leading, guiding, and shepherding. I cannot fail if I humble myself before God, because it is His heart and nature to lead, guide, and shepherd me through this life.

> *"Teach me to do thy will; for thou [art] my God: thy spirit [is] good; lead me into the land of uprightness."* (Psalm 143:10)

"He maketh me to lie down in green pastures: he leadeth me beside the still waters. He restoreth my soul: he leadeth me in the paths of righteousness for his name's sake." (Psalm 23:2-3)

"Howbeit when he, the Spirit of truth, is come, he will guide you into all truth: for he shall not speak of himself; but whatsoever he shall hear, [that] shall he speak: and he will shew you things to come." (John 16:13)

"Now the God of peace, that brought again from the dead our Lord Jesus, that great shepherd of the sheep, through the blood of the everlasting covenant, Make you perfect in every good work to do his will, working in you that which is wellpleasing in his sight, through Jesus Christ; to whom [be] glory for ever and ever. Amen." (Hebrews 13:20-21)

Correcting, chastening, reproving, and consuming fire. As part of His nature as a father, God administers needed correction and burns away everything in my life and heart that stands between me and a closer relationship with Him.

"Behold, happy [is] the man whom God correcteth: therefore despise not thou the chastening of the Almighty." (Job 5:17)

"My son, despise not the chastening of the LORD; neither be weary of his correction: For whom the LORD loveth he correcteth; even as a father the son [in whom] he delighteth." (Proverbs 3:11-12)

"For our God [is] a consuming fire." (Hebrews 12:29)

Directing. God's love for me directs me in the path of right choices when I seek His face and ways.

"In all thy ways acknowledge him, and he shall direct thy paths." (Proverbs 3:6)

"This is what the LORD says—your Redeemer, the Holy One of Israel: "I am the LORD your God, who teaches you what is best for you, who directs you in the way you should go." (Isaiah 48:17 NIV)

Warring, liberating, delivering, and saving. God is not a hands off God, but rather His nature is to be actively and forcefully engaged in the deliverance of those who look to Him. I call on Him at all times with the confidence He will deliver me from trouble.

"He shall call upon me, and I will answer him: I [will be] with him in trouble; I will deliver him, and honour him." (Psalm 91:15)

"The LORD [is] a man of war: the LORD [is] his name." (Exodus 15:3)

"And I saw heaven opened, and behold a white horse; and he that sat upon him [was] called Faithful and True, and in righteousness he doth judge and make war. His eyes [were] as a flame of fire, and on his head [were] many crowns; and he had a name written, that no man knew, but he himself. And he [was] clothed with a vesture dipped in blood: and his name is called The Word of God. And the armies [which were] in heaven followed him upon white horses, clothed in fine linen, white and clean. And out of his mouth goeth a sharp sword, that with it he should smite the nations: and he shall rule them with a rod of iron: and he treadeth the winepress of the fierceness and wrath of Almighty God. And he hath on [his] vesture and on his thigh a name written, KING OF KINGS, AND LORD OF LORDS." (Revelation 19:11-16)

"Who hath saved us, and called [us] with an holy calling, not according to our works, but according to his own purpose and grace, which was given us in Christ Jesus before the world began, But is now made manifest by the appearing of our Saviour Jesus Christ, who hath abolished death, and hath

brought life and immortality to light through the gospel." (2 Timothy 1:9-10)

Sheltering, protecting, shielding, and keeping. God's nature is to protect and to keep His own. No matter what comes against me I take rest in knowing that I belong to God and that He protects me.

"My sheep hear my voice, and I know them, and they follow me: And I give unto them eternal life; and they shall never perish, neither shall any [man] pluck them out of my hand. My Father, which gave [them] me, is greater than all; and no [man] is able to pluck [them] out of my Father's hand. I and [my] Father are one." (John 10:27-30)

"Now unto him that is able to keep you from falling, and to present [you] faultless before the presence of his glory with exceeding joy, to the only wise God our Saviour, [be] glory and majesty, dominion and power, both now and ever. Amen." (Jude 1:24-25)

"But thou, O LORD, [art] a shield for me; my glory, and the lifter up of mine head." (Psalm 3:3)

"He that dwelleth in the secret place of the most High shall abide under the shadow of the Almighty. I will say of the LORD, [He is] my refuge and my fortress: my God; in him will I trust." (Psalm 91:1-2)

Transformed into His likeness

Purifying, refining, pruning, transforming, and regenerating. God's nature is to take me through the sometimes painful process of becoming like Him by removing all that is not like Him from my nature. I not only submit to this process, I ask Him to continue the process until I am fully transformed into His likeness.

"Behold, I have refined thee, but not with silver; I have chosen thee in the furnace of affliction." (Isaiah 48:10)

"I am the true vine, and my Father is the husbandman. Every branch in me that beareth not fruit he taketh away: and every [branch] that beareth fruit, he purgeth it, that it may bring forth more fruit." (John 15:1-2)

"Therefore if any man [be] in Christ, [he is] a new creature: old things are passed away; behold, all things are become new." (2 Corinthians 5:17)

"And God shall wipe away all tears from their eyes; and there shall be no more death, neither sorrow, nor crying, neither shall there be any more pain: for the former things are passed away. And he that sat upon the throne said, Behold, I make all things new. And he said unto me, Write: for these words are true and faithful." (Revelation 21:4-5)

Enlightening, teaching, and revealing. God's nature in assisting the development of man is to reveal the secrets of life. Those who seek enlightenment from themselves or some other power fall into the snare of the fallen angelic light bearer lucifer. Lucifer's light is an illusion and is actually darkness. George Washington Carver, the African-American scientist that developed so many products from the peanut and revitalized agriculture in the southern United States, was said to have had the habit of sitting quietly in God's presence where he waited expectantly for revelation that he then took to his laboratory. I look to God who is the revealer of secrets.

"Surely the Lord GOD will do nothing, but he revealeth his secret unto his servants the prophets." (Amos 3:7)

"That the God of our Lord Jesus Christ, the Father of glory, may give unto you the spirit of wisdom and revelation in the knowledge of him. The eyes of your understanding being enlightened; that ye may know what is the hope of his calling,

and what the riches of the glory of his inheritance in the saints." (Ephesians 1:17-18)

"How that by revelation he made known unto me the mystery; (as I wrote afore in few words. Whereby, when ye read, ye may understand my knowledge in the mystery of Christ). *Which in other ages was not made known unto the sons of men, as it is now revealed unto his holy apostles and prophets by the Spirit; that the Gentiles should be fellow heirs, and of the same body, and partakers of his promise in Christ by the gospel."* (Ephesians 3:3-6)

Warning and pleading. God takes no pleasure in punishing the wicked. Instead, His nature is to warn and plead with us to turn from rebellion and to follow the path of light that leads to Him. I am glad that I listened when God pleaded with my spirit. Now I must be His voice to others.

"Wherefore I will yet plead with you, saith the LORD, and with your children's children will I plead." (Jeremiah 2:9)

"Son of man, I have made thee a watchman unto the house of Israel: therefore hear the word at my mouth, and give them warning from me. When I say unto the wicked, Thou shalt surely die; and thou givest him not warning, nor speakest to warn the wicked from his wicked way, to save his life; the same wicked [man] shall die in his iniquity; but his blood will I require at thine hand. Yet if thou warn the wicked, and he turn not from his wickedness, nor from his wicked way, he shall die in his iniquity; but thou hast delivered thy soul. Again, when a righteous [man] doth turn from his righteous-ness, and commit iniquity, and I lay a stumblingblock before him, he shall die: because thou hast not given him warning, he shall die in his sin, and his righteousness which he hath done shall not be remembered; but his blood will I require at thine hand. Nevertheless if thou warn the righteous [man],

*that the righteous sin not, and he doth not sin, he shall surely
live, because he is warned; also thou hast delivered thy soul."*
(Ezekiel 3:17-21)

Trying and searching. God's nature is to try the reins of my heart and
search my inner depths so that I can see my need of Him and receive His
assistance in living right before Him.

*"I know also, my God, that thou triest the heart, and hast
pleasure in uprightness. As for me, in the uprightness of mine
heart I have willingly offered all these things: and now have I
seen with joy thy people, which are present here, to offer willingly unto thee."* (1 Chronicles 29:17)

*"But, O LORD of hosts, that judgest righteously, that triest
the reins and the heart, let me see thy vengeance on them: for
unto thee have I revealed my cause."* (Jeremiah 11:20)

*"Search me, O God, and know my heart: try me, and know
my thoughts: and see if [there be any] wicked way in me, and
lead me in the way everlasting."* (Psalm 139:23-24)

Renewing and restoring. God's nature is to re-make me in His image
so that I can forever leave behind the things of my past that marred my
life and took me away from Him.

*"Therefore if any man [be] in Christ, [he is] a new creature:
old things are passed away; behold, all things are become new."*
(2 Corinthians 5:17)

*"And I will restore to you the years that the locust hath eaten,
the cankerworm, and the caterpiller, and the palmerworm,
my great army which I sent among you. And ye shall eat in
plenty, and be satisfied, and praise the name of the LORD
your God, that hath dealt wondrously with you: and my
people shall never be ashamed."* (Joel 2:25-26)

Sanctifying and perfecting. God is holy and He sanctifies me so that I can fellowship with Him.

> *"Thou shalt sanctify him therefore; for he offereth the bread of thy God: he shall be holy unto thee: for I the LORD, which sanctify you, [am] holy."* (Leviticus 21:8)

Anointing and strengthening. It is the nature of my strong God to strengthen me so that I can stand in His presence and go and carry out any assignment.

> *"Then he said unto them, Go your way, eat the fat, and drink the sweet, and send portions unto them for whom nothing is prepared: for [this] day [is] holy unto our Lord: neither be ye sorry; for the joy of the LORD is your strength."* (Nehemiah 8:10)

Befriending. God's nature is to do whatever is necessary to draw us into fellowship with Him, if we are willing. I am willing and I seize the opportunity to be a friend of God.

> *"Greater love hath no man than this, that a man lay down his life for his friends. Ye are my friends, if ye do whatsoever I command you. Henceforth I call you not servants; for the servant knoweth not what his lord doeth: but I have called you friends; for all things that I have heard of my Father I have made known unto you."* (John 15:13-15)

Satisfying, rewarding, promoting, exalting, favoring, prospering, blessing, and bountiful. God's nature is to graciously give good gifts to and satisfy those that seek Him. I seek Him and He rewards me and all who will do likewise with blessing upon blessing.

> *"Bring my soul out of prison, that I may praise thy name: the righteous shall compass me about; for thou shalt deal bountifully with me."* (Psalm 142:7)

"The blessing of the LORD, it maketh rich, and he addeth no sorrow with it." (Proverbs 10:22)

"Blessed [is] the man that walketh not in the counsel of the ungodly, nor standeth in the way of sinners, nor sitteth in the seat of the scornful. But his delight [is] in the law of the LORD; and in his law doth he meditate day and night. And he shall be like a tree planted by the rivers of water, that bringeth forth his fruit in his season; his leaf also shall not wither; and whatsoever he doeth shall prosper." (Psalm 1:1-3)

"They shall be abundantly satisfied with the fatness of thy house; and thou shalt make them drink of the river of thy pleasures." (Psalm 36:8)

"For promotion [cometh] neither from the east, nor from the west, nor from the south. But God [is] the judge: he putteth down one, and setteth up another." (Psalm 75:6-7)

"But without faith [it is] impossible to please [him]: for he that cometh to God must believe that he is, and [that] he is a rewarder of them that diligently seek him." (Hebrews 11:6)

God's Nature as Indispensable to Our Lives, Well-being, and Success

His indispensable being is the living Bread of Life, drink, living water, living Word, the way, the door, the life, and the light. This is the nature of God my Father who is light and the Father of lights. The Father Himself loves me. Jesus, the good shepherd, loves me and gave Himself for me. The Holy Spirit, the Helper, whom I do not grieve, sticks closer to me than a brother, abides in me, teaches me all things, and anoints me to do the works of God and to destroy the works of the devil.

The living Bread of Life. Bread is called the staff of life. Unless I partake of the nature of God there can be no real life in me.

"For the bread of God is he which cometh down from heaven, and giveth life unto the world. Then said they unto him, Lord,

evermore give us this bread. And Jesus said unto them, I am the bread of life: he that cometh to me shall never hunger; and he that believeth on me shall never thirst." (John 6:33-35)

"I am that bread of life. Your fathers did eat manna in the wilderness, and are dead. This is the bread which cometh down from heaven, that a man may eat thereof, and not die. I am the living bread which came down from heaven: if any man eat of this bread, he shall live for ever: and the bread that I will give is my flesh, which I will give for the life of the world." (John 6:48-51)

Drink and living water. Our world's surface is mostly water. Without drinking water or water-based fluids we would die after three or more days. Where there is no water the earth itself becomes barren. God's nature is the living water necessary to sustain my life and to give me life in the Spirit with Him.

"Then Jesus said unto them, Verily, verily, I say unto you, Except ye eat the flesh of the Son of man, and drink his blood, ye have no life in you. Whoso eateth my flesh, and drinketh my blood, hath eternal life; and I will raise him up at the last day. For my flesh is meat indeed, and my blood is drink indeed. He that eateth my flesh, and drinketh my blood, dwelleth in me, and I in him." (John 6:53-56)

"O LORD, the hope of Israel, all that forsake thee shall be ashamed, [and] they that depart from me shall be written in the earth, because they have forsaken the LORD, the fountain of living waters." (Jeremiah 17:13)

Living Word. God's word is not a dead letter. The life of His nature in His word also makes me live when I receive it and act on it with faith.

"For you have been born again, not of perishable seed, but of imperishable, through the living and enduring word of God." (1 Peter 1:23 NIV)

"In the beginning was the Word, and the Word was with God, and the Word was God. He was with God in the beginning. Through him all things were made; without him nothing was made that has been made. In him was life, and that life was the light of all mankind." (John 1:1-4)

The way, the door, and the life. Although there are religions and philosophies that claim to be another way to God, Jesus Christ the Son of God is the only way to God the Father and to eternal life. He is the sole portal for entry into heaven. Anything else is a fraud and leads to death and separation from God.

"Jesus saith unto him, I am the way, the truth, and the life: no man cometh unto the Father, but by me." (John 14:6)

"I am the door: by me if any man enter in, he shall be saved, and shall go in and out, and find pasture." (John 10:9)

The light. This is the nature of God my Father who is light and the Father of lights. God is light and the Father of the angels of light. His desire is to transform me into a being of light for fellowship with Him. Apart from Him this is impossible.

"This then is the message which we have heard of him, and declare unto you, that God is light, and in him is no darkness at all." (1 John 1:5)

"Every good gift and every perfect gift is from above, and cometh down from the Father of lights, with whom is no variableness, neither shadow of turning." (James 1:17)

"And after six days Jesus taketh Peter, James, and John his brother, and bringeth them up into an high mountain apart, and was transfigured before them: and his face did shine as the sun, and his raiment was white as the light." (Matthew 17:1-2)

The Father Himself loves me. God is not an angry judge seeking whom He may judge and destroy. God's nature of love drove Him to find a way, at an extremely high price, to bring me and all who reciprocate His love back into a relationship of fellowship with Him for eternity.

> *"He that loveth not knoweth not God; for God is love. In this was manifested the love of God toward us, because that God sent his only begotten Son into the world, that we might live through him. Herein is love, not that we loved God, but that he loved us, and sent his Son [to be] the propitiation for our sins."* (1 John 4:8-10)

> *"For the Father himself loveth you, because ye have loved me, and have believed that I came out from God."* (John 16:27)

Jesus, the good shepherd, loves me and gave Himself for me. The gap between God and man is far greater than that between a man and the sheep he may herd and care for. Yet, the nature of God's love for me was that He not only cared for me but took on the body of a mortal man, through birth, so that He could die for me, pay the penalty for the sins of the world, and redeem me and all who receive Him to Himself for eternity.

> *"I am the good shepherd: the good shepherd giveth his life for the sheep."* (John 10:11)

> *"I am crucified with Christ: nevertheless I live; yet not I, but Christ liveth in me: and the life which I now live in the flesh I live by the faith of the Son of God, who loved me, and gave himself for me."* (Galatians 2:20)

The Holy Spirit, the Helper, whom I do not grieve, sticks closer to me than a brother, abides in me, teaches me all things, and anoints me to do the works of God and to destroy the works of the devil. The presence of God the Holy Spirit around me and in me is proof that Jesus Christ rose from the dead and is who He said He was—the one foretold in prophesy and promised by God the Father. Having received such a precious gift, it is my desire to allow the life of Christ to be lived through me and to do nothing that grates on that holy presence within me.

"And I will pray the Father, and he shall give you another Comforter, that he may abide with you for ever;   [Even] the Spirit of truth; whom the world cannot receive, because it seeth him not, neither knoweth him: but ye know him; for he dwelleth with you, and shall be in you." (John 14:16-17)

"And grieve not the holy Spirit of God, whereby ye are sealed unto the day of redemption." (Ephesians 4:30)

CHAPTER 4
I AM SANCTIFIED BY THE WORK
OF GOD AND I ABIDE IN HIM

*Lord, I seek your face, heart, and voice, and I find You. I see the Lord.
I linger with You in Your glory light and am transformed into Your image
as all within me that is not like You is consumed by the light of Your glory
and Your holy fire. I am a man after God's own heart. I am a worshipper
and have found the key of David that opens a door into the throne room of
the manifest presence of God. By Your grace and power Yahweh Mikkadesh,
God my sanctifier, I commit to keeping Your commandments, doing all Your
will, and to walking in Jesus' commandment of love. I pledge obedience and
singleness of heart. My old life and selfish, prideful, errant nature is crucified
with Christ. It is no longer I that live, but Christ. The ideal servant of the
Lord is reproduced in me. I am washed in the Blood of Jesus from all sin and
condemnation and I walk continually in holiness by the power of the Holy
Ghost. I consecrate myself to and abide in God and revel in the ecstasy of
His intimate presence. Yahweh Shammah, the Lord is present, is with me. I
am kept clean daily by self-examination, the renewing of my mind, and the
washing of the water of the Word of God. I take captive every thought that
attempts to exalt itself above the knowledge of Christ. I do not sin with my
eyes; I flee from evil, I renounce ungodly soul ties and affections, and I do not
dwell in places of unrighteousness. I do not consider, meditate upon, or act
out ungodly pleasure. No ungodly addiction has control of me, and when the
prince of this world comes he finds no place in me.*

Lord, I seek your face, heart, and voice, and I find You. I am determined to seek God and to know Him. It is a continual Christian discipline and not a once and off commitment. The reward is that I get to find Him, lay hold on Him, and discover more about Him and His ways.

> *"And ye shall seek me, and find [me], when ye shall search for me with all your heart."* (Jeremiah 29:13)

> *"Seek the LORD and his strength, seek his face continually."* (1 Chronicles 16:11)

> *"[When thou saidst], Seek ye my face; my heart said unto thee, Thy face, LORD, will I seek."* (Psalm 27:8)

I see the Lord. The Bible is replete with scriptures detailing the experiences of old and new testament believers as they saw God in various ways. Although many were the experiences of individuals, some involved two or many more people. That experience is also for you and me in our time because God has not changed.

> *"In the year that king Uzziah died I saw also the Lord sitting upon a throne, high and lifted up, and his train filled the temple."* (Isaiah 6:1)

> *"Blessed [are] the pure in heart: for they shall see God."* (Matthew 5:8)

> *"He that hath my commandments, and keepeth them, he it is that loveth me: and he that loveth me shall be loved of my Father, and I will love him, and will manifest myself to him."* (John 14:21)

I linger with You in Your glory light and am transformed into Your image as all within me that is not like You is consumed by the light of Your glory and Your holy fire. God tests the hearts. He desires people who long for Him and who do not easily turn away from His presence. Our modern twenty-first century world has many distractions, devices, news, and entertainment sources that compete for our attention. I marvel at drivers who take their eyes from the road to read or send a text message from their smart phones. I also see pedestrians crossing streets without an awareness of traffic because they are in another place with music filling their ears from headphones or ear buds, or are involved in an animated, and sometimes loud, conversation on their cell phones. Some believers of centuries past spent hours upon hours of their time seeking the face of God in prayer or contemplation. My challenge is to simplify life, prioritize, and value time spent on a regular basis seeking God's face and the light of His glory. In the process, I will be changed into His likeness from one level to the next higher level. Then, others will know that I have been with God.

I will be changed into His likeness

"But we all, with open face beholding as in a glass the glory of the Lord, are changed into the same image from glory to glory, [even] as by the Spirit of the Lord." (2 Corinthians 3:18)

"And it came to pass, as Moses entered into the tabernacle, the cloudy pillar descended, and stood [at] the door of the tabernacle, and [the LORD] talked with Moses. And all the people saw the cloudy pillar stand [at] the tabernacle door: and all the people rose up and worshipped, every man [in] his tent door. And the LORD spake unto Moses face to face, as a man speaketh unto his friend. And he turned again into the camp: but his servant Joshua, the son of Nun, a young man, departed not out of the tabernacle." (Exodus 33:9-11)

"For our God [is] a consuming fire." (Hebrews 12:29)

"But if we walk in the light, as he is in the light, we have fellowship one with another, and the blood of Jesus Christ his Son cleanseth us from all sin." (1 John 1:7)

I am a man after God's own heart. I want God to say of me that, like David of old, I am a man after His own heart, and that He can trust me to do all that He shows me to do.

"And when he had removed him, he raised up unto them David to be their king; to whom also he gave testimony, and said, I have found David the [son] of Jesse, a man after mine own heart, which shall fulfil all my will." (Acts 13:22)

I am a worshipper and have found the key of David that opens a door into the throne room of the manifest presence of God. David was a psalmist and a worshipper. That was his identity as a nobody rejected by his own father and brothers when God sent the prophet Samuel to Jesse to anoint one of his sons to be king in place of Saul. It was also his identity while he was king. As king, David set up an elaborate system of 24-hour praise and worship that was conducted on a daily basis at his temporary tent structure tabernacle, and later at his son Solomon's temple. The death and resurrection of Jesus Christ forever changed the system of worship with the once and for all time sacrifice of the blood of the Lamb of God. Whereas the high priest could enter the holiest part of the temple once a year after rituals of cleansing and sacrifice, I have an access that has been paid for by my savior and redeemer. Nevertheless, I must not take God lightly. God is everywhere and lives inside me. I have this treasure in a jar of clay, that is to say in my body. I can facilitate entry into the experience of the manifest presence of God by the acceptable sacrifice of the blood of Jesus and the tools of thanksgiving, praise, and worship presented from a heart that is broken and contrite. This was the key in the life of David and his relationship with God.

I can facilitate entry into the experience of the manifest presence of God by the blood of Jesus and the tools of thanksgiving, praise, and worship

"*Serve the LORD with gladness: come before his presence with singing. Know ye that the LORD he [is] God: [it is] he [that] hath made us, and not we ourselves; [we are] his people, and the sheep of his pasture. Enter into his gates with thanksgiving, [and] into his courts with praise: be thankful unto him, [and] bless his name."* (Psalm 100:2-4)

"O Lord, open thou my lips; and my mouth shall shew forth thy praise. For thou desirest not sacrifice; else would I give it: thou delightest not in burnt offering. The sacrifices of God are a broken spirit: a broken and a contrite heart, O God, thou wilt not despise." (Psalm 51:15-17)

"I will praise the name of God with a song, and will magnify him with thanksgiving. This also shall please the LORD better than an ox or bullock that hath horns and hoofs." (Psalm 69:30-31)

"Let us therefore come boldly unto the throne of grace, that we may obtain mercy, and find grace to help in time of need." (Hebrews 4:16)

"By him therefore let us offer the sacrifice of praise to God continually, that is, the fruit of our lips giving thanks to his name." (Hebrews 13:15)

By Your grace and power Yahweh Mikkadesh, God my sanctifier, I commit to keeping Your commandments, doing all Your will, and to walking in Jesus' commandment of love. Without God I can do nothing. Without God I can't even keep His commandments or, less so, all of the laws of men. I might live a good life and be recognized as a good person in the community, but I need the grace that goes beyond my sinful nature and I need the power of God to sanctify me and cause me to live in a way that is thoroughly pleasing to Him.

"Speak thou also unto the children of Israel, saying, Verily my sabbaths ye shall keep: for it [is] a sign between me and you throughout your generations; that [ye] may know that I [am] the LORD that doth sanctify you." (Exodus 31:13)

"If ye keep my commandments, ye shall abide in my love; even as I have kept my Father's commandments, and abide in his love." (John 15:10)

"This is my commandment, that ye love one another, as I have loved you." (John 15:12)

"Now the God of peace, that brought again from the dead our Lord Jesus, that great shepherd of the sheep, through the blood of the everlasting covenant, make you perfect in every good work to do his will, working in you that which is wellpleasing in his sight, through Jesus Christ; to whom [be] glory for ever and ever. Amen." (Hebrews 13:20-21)

I pledge obedience and singleness of heart. God is looking for perfect hearts. My imperfect performance can be covered by His grace and the blood of Jesus if my heart is perfect toward Him, I am quick to be sorry for any sin, and then get back to walking with Him by the power of the Holy Spirit.

"With my whole heart have I sought thee: O let me not wander from thy commandments. Thy word have I hid in mine heart, that I might not sin against thee." (Psalm 119:10-11)

"I will behave myself wisely in a perfect way. O when wilt thou come unto me? I will walk within my house with a perfect heart." (Psalm 101:2)

God is looking for perfect hearts

My old life and selfish, prideful, errant nature is crucified with Christ. It is no longer I that live, but Christ. I reckon my self-pleasing, arrogant, easy to take offense, and erring nature to be dead to the things that would stir it up. By faith, I allow and even plead for Christ to live His life through me. It is not just about asking myself "what would Jesus do?" I need divine assistance to live the life that is pleasing to God. Anything less is the road that my good intentions, but poor follow through, would lead to.

> *"For ye are dead, and your life is hid with Christ in God."* (Colossians 3:3)

> *"I am crucified with Christ: nevertheless I live; yet not I, but Christ liveth in me: and the life which I now live in the flesh I live by the faith of the Son of God, who loved me, and gave himself for me."* (Galatians 2:20)

> *"And they that are Christ's have crucified the flesh with the affections and lusts."* (Galatians 5:24)

The ideal servant of the Lord is reproduced in me. My prayer to God is "all of You and none of me." As God's Spirit and nature are imparted to me, and I determine to walk in that impartation, I become more like Him so that people see His likeness in me, rather than the old Louis with all of his failings.

> *"But no weapon that is formed against you shall prosper, and every tongue that shall rise against you in judgment you shall show to be in the wrong. This [peace, righteousness, security, triumph over opposition] is the heritage of the servants of the Lord [those in whom the ideal Servant of the Lord is reproduced]; this is the righteousness or the vindication which they obtain from Me [this is that which I impart to them as their justification], says the Lord."* (Isaiah 54:17 AMP)

I am washed in the Blood of Jesus from all sin and condemnation and I walk continually in holiness by the power of the Holy Ghost. It is not that I have never messed up. In fact, I am downright embarrassed all by myself when I recall incidents from my distant and sometimes painfully near past. But God has made a way, at an extremely high cost, for me to be free of condemnation for my past and to live a life that pleases Him day by day, hour by hour, and moment by moment.

"But if we walk in the light, as he is in the light, we have fellowship one with another, and the blood of Jesus Christ his Son cleanseth us from all sin." (1 John 1:7)

"[There is] therefore now no condemnation to them which are in Christ Jesus, who walk not after the flesh, but after the Spirit." (Romans 8:1)

I consecrate myself to and abide in God and revel in the ecstasy of His intimate presence. Thirty-five years ago in Africa, a missionary stood in front of me, ignoring others present, and sang the words of Psalm 25 verse one as he strummed on his guitar. Afterwards, some asked what was going on. That man was challenging me, out of many others present, to consecrate my life to God. It has been a journey, but my will is to consecrate myself to God and to enter into the delights of God's presence, now, in this life.

"[A Psalm] of David.] Unto thee, O LORD, do I lift up my soul." (Psalm 25:1)

"I beseech you therefore, brethren, by the mercies of God, that ye present your bodies a living sacrifice, holy, acceptable unto God, [which is] your reasonable service." (Romans 12:1)

"Thou wilt shew me the path of life: in thy presence [is] fulness of joy; at thy right hand [there are] pleasures for evermore." (Psalm 16:11)

Yahweh Shammah, the Lord is present, is with me. Emmanuel, God with us, is here with me. I want to make God comfortable as He keeps company with me. I want to live in the reality of God's constant presence and not consign Him to the shelf until some better time or for when I am in a jam and need immediate help from on high.

"Yea, though I walk through the valley of the shadow of death, I will fear no evil: for thou [art] with me; thy rod and thy staff they comfort me." (Psalm 23:4)

"The distance all around will be 18,000 cubits. And the name of the city from that time on will be: the Lord is there." (Ezekiel 48:35 NIV)

I am kept clean daily by self-examination, the renewing of my mind, and the washing of the water of the Word of God. There is a proactive part of my walk with God that I am responsible for initiating. I take the free will that God has given me and discipline it to seek God, His word, and ways, and believe that God will do the rest to accomplish the renewal of my spirit.

"Finally, brethren, whatsoever things are true, whatsoever things [are] honest, whatsoever things [are] just, whatsoever things [are] pure, whatsoever things [are] lovely, whatsoever things [are] of good report; if [there be] any virtue, and if [there be] any praise, think on these things." (Philippians 4:8)

"And be renewed in the spirit of your mind." (Ephesians 4:23)

"For which cause we faint not; but though our outward man perish, yet the inward [man] is renewed day by day." (2 Corinthians 4:16)

"Having therefore these promises, dearly beloved, let us cleanse ourselves from all filthiness of the flesh and spirit, perfecting holiness in the fear of God." (2 Corinthians 7:1)

"All scripture [is] given by inspiration of God, and [is] profitable for doctrine, for reproof, for correction, for instruction in righteousness: That the man of God may be perfect, thoroughly furnished unto all good works." (2 Timothy 3:16-17)

I take captive every thought that attempts to exalt itself above the knowledge of Christ. We live in a media and communications age. Messages from the culture of this day are constantly bombarding me. In addition, my own natural bent is wayward. Therefore, I actively contend for the purity of my thought life, judge, and cast down every philosophy, compromise, thought, and imagining that would seek to trump the knowledge of Christ in my life.

> *"Casting down imaginations, and every high thing that exalteth itself against the knowledge of God, and bringing into captivity every thought to the obedience of Christ."* (2 Corinthians 10:5)

I do not sin with my eyes; I flee from evil, I renounce ungodly soul ties and affections, and I do not dwell in places of unrighteousness. I do not consider, meditate upon, or act out ungodly pleasure. Joyce Meyer, whose ministry my wife and I follow on the television and occasionally by attending her conferences, has often said "where the mind goes the man follows." I have made up my mind to consciously reject thoughts or actions that displease God—and I rely upon God for the grace and strength to implement that deal that I made with myself to live a life that honors God even when no one else is looking. There are no secrets where God is concerned.

> *"I made a covenant with mine eyes; why then should I think upon a maid?"* (Job 31:1)

> *"But I say unto you, That whosoever looketh on a woman to lust after her hath committed adultery with her already in his heart."* (Matthew 5:28)

> *"I will set no wicked thing before mine eyes: I hate the work of them that turn aside; [it] shall not cleave to me."* (Psalm 101:3)

> *"For the grace of God that bringeth salvation hath appeared to all men, teaching us that, denying ungodliness and worldly lusts, we should live soberly, righteously, and godly, in this present world."* (Titus 2:11-12)

> *"But every man is tempted, when he is drawn away of his own lust, and enticed. Then when lust hath conceived, it bringeth*

forth sin: and sin, when it is finished, bringeth forth death."
(James 1:14-15)

*"Know ye not that your bodies are the members of Christ?
Shall I then take the members of Christ, and make them the
members of an harlot? God forbid. What? Know ye not that
he which is joined to an harlot is one body? For two, saith he,
shall be one flesh."* (1Corinthians 6:15-16)

No ungodly addiction has control of me, and when the prince of this
world comes he finds no place in me. I have had pet sins and secret sins
that caused me shame and with which I struggled for mastery of my
own self. God is faithful to deliver me when I call upon Him for help.
If we truly examine ourselves and seek God's assistance in breaking the
chains of additions and habits that drag us down, then we can reach the
point when the temptations that satan tries to surprise us with no longer
have power over us. We can become so free that satan and his demonic
cohorts cannot establish a beachhead in the battle for our allegiance or
occupy a secret chamber in our hearts from which to extend the control
of darkness in our lives.

*"Hereafter I will not talk much with you: for the prince of this
world cometh, and hath nothing in me."* (John 14:30)

*"Who can understand [his] errors? cleanse thou me from secret
[faults]. Keep back thy servant also from presumptuous [sins];
let them not have dominion over me: then shall I be upright,
and I shall be innocent from the great transgression."* (Psalm
19:12-13)

CHAPTER 5
I AM A WHOLLY DEVOTED
FOLLOWER OF CHRIST JESUS

Jesus is El Yeshuati and Yahweh Shua, the God of my salvation and redemption. I unreservedly believe and follow the revelation God my Father gave of Himself through the manifestation in human flesh of the person of Jesus. There is salvation in none other. As a true disciple of Christ Jesus, I take up my cross, in disregard of self-will, and follow Him. I am strong in the LORD and of good courage. Jesus is Yahweh Shalom, the Lord our peace. I have the peace of God. I do not fear man or the principalities and powers of satan's kingdom. I am in reverential awe of God. I don't halt between two opinions or vacillate between going God's way and trying to obtain success by going man's way.

The Revelation of Jesus

Jesus is El Yeshuati and Yahweh Shua, the God of my salvation and redemption. I recognize and worship Jesus Christ as God my Savior who redeemed me from a state of sin and has made possible my fellowship with God now and for eternity.

> *"The LORD [is] my strength and song, and he is become my salvation: he [is] my God, and I will prepare him an habitation; my father's God, and I will exalt him."* (Exodus 15:2)

"...and all flesh shall know that I the LORD am thy Saviour and thy Redeemer, the mighty One of Jacob." (Isaiah 49:26)

"The LORD liveth; and blessed [be] my rock; and let the God of my salvation be exalted." (Psalm 18:46)

"Behold, God [is] my salvation; I will trust, and not be afraid: for the LORD JEHOVAH [is] my strength and [my] song; he also is become my salvation. Therefore with joy shall ye draw water out of the wells of salvation." (Isaiah 12:2-3)

"For the grace of God that bringeth salvation hath appeared to all men, Teaching us that, denying ungodliness and worldly lusts, we should live soberly, righteously, and godly, in this present world; looking for that blessed hope, and the glorious appearing of the great God and our Saviour Jesus Christ; who gave himself for us, that he might redeem us from all iniquity, and purify unto himself a peculiar people, zealous of good works." (Titus 2:11-14)

"And we have seen and do testify that the Father sent the Son [to be] the Saviour of the world." (1 John 4:14)

Love Bond with the Revealed Christ

I unreservedly believe and follow the revelation God my Father gave of Himself through the manifestation in human flesh of the person of Jesus. There is salvation in none other. As a true disciple of Christ Jesus, I take up my cross, in disregard of self-will, and follow Him. I unconditionally acknowledge and accept the revelation of God in the flesh and blood person of Jesus. There is no other way to heaven or to please God my Father. I willingly follow Jesus as one of His disciples. In doing so I put aside personal ambition and preferences and make myself available to Him.

I unconditionally acknowledge and accept the revelation of God in the flesh and blood person of Jesus

"Then said Jesus unto his disciples, If any man will come after me, let him deny himself, and take up his cross, and follow me." (Matthew 16:24)

"Search the scriptures; for in them ye think ye have eternal life: and they are they which testify of me." (John 5:39)

I am strong in the LORD and of good courage. I am not afraid of the challenges that may lie ahead of me because I draw my strength and resolve from the Lord. I rest in His promise to always be with me.

"Have not I commanded thee? Be strong and of a good courage; be not afraid, neither be thou dismayed: for the LORD thy God is with thee whithersoever thou goest." (Joshua 1:9)

Jesus is Yahweh Shalom, the Lord our peace. I have the peace of God. I have made peace with God through Jesus Christ and the peace of God has come over me.

"Now the God of peace, that brought again from the dead our Lord Jesus, that great shepherd of the sheep, through the blood of the everlasting covenant, make you perfect in every good work to do his will, working in you that which is wellpleasing in his sight, through Jesus Christ; to whom be glory for ever and ever. Amen." (Hebrews 13:20-21)

"Peace I leave with you, my peace I give unto you: not as the world giveth, give I unto you. Let not your heart be troubled, neither let it be afraid." (John 14:27)

"Therefore being justified by faith, we have peace with God through our Lord Jesus Christ." (Romans 5:1)

I do not fear man or the principalities and powers of satan's kingdom. I don't have to fear people or the evil spirits that may align themselves with them against me because God has given me His Spirit.

"For we wrestle not against flesh and blood, but against principalities, against powers, against the rulers of the darkness of this world, against spiritual wickedness in high [places]." (Ephesians 6:12)

"For God hath not given us the spirit of fear; but of power, and of love, and of a sound mind." (2 Timothy 1:7)

I am in reverential awe of God. I am amazed and am in reverential awe of all that God is, therefore I love Him, desire to serve Him, and I want to live a life that is pleasing to Him as a way to honor Him.

"And now, Israel, what doth the LORD thy God require of thee, but to fear the LORD thy God, to walk in all his ways, and to love him, and to serve the LORD thy God with all thy heart and with all thy soul." (Deuteronomy 10:12)

"God is greatly to be feared in the assembly of the saints, and to be had in reverence of all [them that are] about him." (Psalm 89:7)

"Therefore, since we are receiving a kingdom that cannot be shaken, let us be thankful, and so worship God acceptably with reverence and awe." (Hebrews 12:28 NIV)

I don't halt between two opinions or vacillate between going God's way and trying to obtain success by going man's way. I have made my decision. I have decided to follow the Lord all the days of my life. I am careful to seek God's counsel and not trust or rely on my own ideas or the advice of those who don't acknowledge God as Lord of their lives.

"And Elijah came unto all the people, and said, How long halt ye between two opinions? If the LORD [be] God, follow him: but if Baal, [then] follow him. And the people answered him not a word." (1 Kings 18:21)

"Thus saith the LORD; Cursed [be] the man that trusteth in man, and maketh flesh his arm, and whose heart departeth

from the LORD. For he shall be like the heath in the desert, and shall not see when good cometh; but shall inhabit the parched places in the wilderness, [in] a salt land and not inhabited. Blessed [is] the man that trusteth in the LORD, and whose hope the LORD is." (Jeremiah 17:5-7)

"Trust in the LORD with all thine heart; and lean not unto thine own understanding. In all thy ways acknowledge him, and he shall direct thy paths." (Proverbs 3:5-6)

CHAPTER 6
I PROCLAIM THE WHOLE, TRUE GOSPEL OF THE PERSON AND WORK OF CHRIST JESUS

I boldly and effectively proclaim to the nations the name of the LORD and His good news that the Kingdom of God is near, that we have entrance by faith through repentance from sin and by confession of and belief in the person and work of Christ Jesus, His sin atoning shed blood, His substitutionary death on the cross, His resurrection, and the indwelling of the Holy Spirit, by which things we are saved from the kingdom of darkness, reconciled to God by His work of grace, and restored to our original and rightful places as His children, heirs of His Kingdom, and as co-rulers of the earth.

Proclaiming the Creed

I boldly and effectively proclaim to the nations the name of the LORD and His good news that the Kingdom of God is near, that we have entrance by faith through repentance from sin and by confession of and belief in the person and work of Christ Jesus. I have had the privilege of living in or traveling to over 60 countries for business or pleasure. I try to declare and share the gospel of Jesus Christ wherever I go, including where I send my financial support to other witnesses of the gospel. These are fellow witnesses of salvation through the finished work of Jesus Christ and of a person's open confession of belief in His name, coupled with sorrow for past sins and a determination to live for Christ by the help of God the Holy Spirit.

"And he said unto them, Go ye into all the world, and preach the gospel to every creature." (Mark 16:15)

"But ye shall receive power, after that the Holy Ghost is come upon you: and ye shall be witnesses unto me both in Jerusalem, and in all Judaea, and in Samaria, and unto the uttermost part of the earth." (Acts 1:8)

"But what saith it? The word is nigh thee, even in thy mouth, and in thy heart: that is, the word of faith, which we preach; that if thou shalt confess with thy mouth the Lord Jesus, and shalt believe in thine heart that God hath raised him from the dead, thou shalt be saved. For with the heart man believeth unto righteousness; and with the mouth confession is made unto salvation." (Romans 10:8-10)

"Jesus saith unto him, I am the way, the truth, and the life: no man cometh unto the Father, but by me." (John 14:6)

"Who, being in the form of God, thought it not robbery to be equal with God: but made himself of no reputation, and took upon him the form of a servant, and was made in the likeness of men: and being found in fashion as a man, he humbled himself, and became obedient unto death, even the death of the cross. Wherefore God also hath highly exalted him, and given him a name which is above every name: that at the name of Jesus every knee should bow, of [things] in heaven, and [things] in earth, and [things] under the earth; and [that] every tongue should confess that Jesus Christ [is] Lord, to the glory of God the Father." (Philippians 2:6-11)

"And without controversy great is the mystery of godliness: God was manifest in the flesh, justified in the Spirit, seen of angels, preached unto the Gentiles, believed on in the world, received up into glory." (1 Timothy 3:16)

"Now after that John was put in prison, Jesus came into Galilee, preaching the gospel of the kingdom of God, And saying, The time is fulfilled, and the kingdom of God is at hand: repent ye, and believe the gospel." (Mark 1:14-15)

"And I heard a loud voice saying in heaven, Now is come salvation, and strength, and the kingdom of our God, and the power of his Christ: for the accuser of our brethren is cast down, which accused them before our God day and night." (Revelation 12:10)

His sin atoning shed blood, His substitutionary death on the cross, His resurrection, and the indwelling of the Holy Spirit, by which things we are saved from the kingdom of darkness, reconciled to God by His work of grace, and restored to our original and rightful places as His children, heirs of His Kingdom, and as co-rulers of the earth. I share the whole gospel of the love and grace of God through Christ Jesus. It is an inestimable gift to be freely received. Yet, I share that good news with the dreadful knowledge that those who choose to ignore or reject this great gift have no other way to escape the judgment that will come on a rebellious world.

An inestimable gift

"And he is the propitiation for our sins: and not for ours only, but also for [the sins of] the whole world." (1 John 2:2)

"But God, who is rich in mercy, for his great love wherewith he loved us, Even when we were dead in sins, hath quickened us together with Christ, (by grace ye are saved;) *and hath raised [us] up together, and made [us] sit together in heavenly [places] in Christ Jesus: that in the ages to come he might shew the exceeding riches of his grace in [his] kindness toward us through Christ Jesus. For by grace are ye saved through faith; and that not of yourselves: [it is] the gift of God: not of works, lest any man should boast."* (Ephesians 2:4-9)

"But ye are not in the flesh, but in the Spirit, if so be that the Spirit of God dwell in you. Now if any man have not the Spirit of Christ, he is none of his. And if Christ be in you, the body is dead because of sin; but the Spirit is life because of righteousness. But if the Spirit of him that raised up Jesus from the dead dwell in you, he that raised up Christ from the dead shall also quicken your mortal bodies by his Spirit that dwelleth in you." (Romans 8:9-11)

"And they sung a new song, saying, Thou art worthy to take the book, and to open the seals thereof: for thou wast slain, and hast redeemed us to God by thy blood out of every kindred, and tongue, and people, and nation; And hast made us unto our God kings and priests: and we shall reign on the earth." (Revelation 5:9-10)

"How shall we escape, if we neglect so great salvation; which at the first began to be spoken by the Lord, and was confirmed unto us by them that heard him?" (Hebrews 2:3)

CHAPTER 7
I ENGAGE IN SPIRITUAL WARFARE AND CONQUER THROUGH GOD

The power of witchcraft, demonic strongholds, curses, and of the curse over my life is broken, because Jesus took the curse on Himself that I would have The Blessing. You are Yahweh Eloheka, the God who brings me out of slavery and I stand fast in that liberty. Jesus is Yahweh Nissi, God my banner – the Lord is my victory and Yahweh Sabaoth, the Lord of angelic heavenly armies. I resist the devil and he flees. I bind and cast down to the pit demonic strongmen, spiritual principalities, and rulers of darkness in high places. I restore the foundations, repair breeches, and build up God ordained walls to keep out the enemies of our souls. I bring the light of God where there was darkness and deliver many from the bondage of captivity to life in the light and freedom of the Kingdom of God. In my life and in the lives of others whose souls have been scared by others or by our own wrong choices and habits, I, by the Spirit of God, bring recovery of that which was damaged or stolen, deliverance from enslavement, and the gifts of restoration, healing, and reconciliation. I am more than a conqueror through Him that loved me.

You are Yahweh Elohay, the Lord my God who cares for me. Nothing shall separate me from the love of Christ. I rule and reign with Christ now, in this time, and in the ages to come. My enemies are defeated whether they be in the flesh or from the spirit realm. The devil, his demons, the kingdom of darkness, and the world system are defeated. The power of sin and of

condemnation over my life and destiny is broken. In the power and author-
ity of Jesus name I speak to the mountains of debt, diabetes, back problems,
and excess weight and command them to go! Debt is defeated and cancelled.
Lack and the spirit of poverty are defeated. The devourer is rebuked. The
thief is defeated. You are Yahweh Rophe, God my healer, therefore diabetes,
obesity, arthritis, allergies, back problems, and all sicknesses are defeated. I
bind and take authority over all the power of the enemy in Jesus' name. You
are Yahweh Gmolah, the Lord of recompense who rewards and compensates
Your children. You restore all that has been stolen from me and give me a
recompense of double that which was stolen. Your justice, when the thief is
caught, restores to me seven times what was stolen.

Battleground Earth! Spirit Forces in Conflict

The power of witchcraft, demonic strongholds, curses, and of the curse
over my life is broken, because Jesus took the curse on Himself that I would
have the Blessing. I recognize that I have a parallel battle in the dimension
of the spirit. I fight against the weapons that my adversaries attempt to
use to halt or slow my progress in the things of God. In my ignorance
and foolish choices, I may have opened the door to the power of curses.
However, Jesus Christ has redeemed me from curses and has given me
mighty weapons in the spirit to pull down strongholds in my life and in
the lives of others.

> *"Christ hath redeemed us from the curse of the law, being*
> *made a curse for us: for it is written, Cursed [is] every one that*
> *hangeth on a tree: that the blessing of Abraham might come*
> *on the Gentiles through Jesus Christ; that we might receive the*
> *promise of the Spirit through faith."* (Galatians 3:13-14)

> "(For the weapons of our warfare [are] not carnal, but
> mighty through God to the pulling down of strong holds.)"
> (2 Corithians 10:4)

You are Yahweh Eloheka, the God who brings me out of slavery and I
stand fast in that liberty. The habits and inclinations to which I was once
enslaved are broken because God has brought me out of that bondage.

He keeps me in liberty as I will to remain free by His power and my ongoing decisions to make right choices.

"I [am] the LORD thy God, which have brought thee out of the land of Egypt, out of the house of bondage." (Exodus 20:2)

"[Then] beware lest thou forget the LORD, which brought thee forth out of the land of Egypt, from the house of bondage." (Deuteronomy 6:12)

"Stand fast therefore in the liberty wherewith Christ hath made us free, and be not entangled again with the yoke of bondage." (Galatians 5:1)

Jesus is Yahweh Nissi, God my banner – the Lord is my victory and Yahweh Sabaoth, the Lord of angelic heavenly armies. Jesus has always been the leader of the armies of heaven. When He was born as a man He set aside His glory. On the cross of Calvary He could have called for angels to save Him, but He chose to fulfill the prophesies of His being the Lamb of God and willingly laid down His life in obedience to the will of God the Father that He fulfill the purpose for which He came for my salvation and redemption. When He returns again it will be with all of the power of the Godhead and with angelic armies. In the meantime, I can draw upon His power and His willingness to dispatch angelic assistance to aid me to gain victories now in this life.

I can draw upon His power

"And Moses built an altar, and called the name of it Jehovahnissi." (Exodus 17:15)

"And as Esaias said before, Except the Lord of Sabaoth had left us a seed, we had been as Sodoma, and been made like unto Gomorrha." (Romans 9:29)

"And it came to pass, when Joshua was by Jericho, that he lifted up his eyes and looked, and, behold, there stood a man

over against him with his sword drawn in his hand: and Joshua went unto him, and said unto him, [Art] thou for us, or for our adversaries? And he said, Nay; but [as] captain of the host of the LORD am I now come. And Joshua fell on his face to the earth, and did worship, and said unto him, What saith my lord unto his servant?" (Joshua 5:13-14)

"And I saw heaven opened, and behold a white horse; and he that sat upon him [was] called Faithful and True, and in righteousness he doth judge and make war." (Revelation 19:11)

I Battle Evil Spirits Too

I resist the devil and he flees. Although I don't have authority to give orders to the angels of God, because they only answer to Him and do His will, I share in the victory of Christ Jesus over satan and his rebel angels. I resist the devil and command him and his demons to flee and to give up people and territory they have taken—and they must obey.

"Submit yourselves therefore to God. Resist the devil, and he will flee from you." (James 4:7)

"Ye are of God, little children, and have overcome them: because greater is he that is in you, than he that is in the world." (1 John 4:4)

I bind and cast down to the pit demonic strongmen, spiritual principalities, and rulers of darkness in high places. The kingdom that satan rules is organized, hierarchical, and territorial. Nevertheless, Jesus has given me power over the kingdom of darkness. I use that power and authority to victoriously battle that enemy and I don't get distracted by the people satan has influenced to work in concert with his dark kingdom.

"For we wrestle not against flesh and blood, but against principalities, against powers, against the rulers of the darkness of this world, against spiritual wickedness in high [places]." (Ephesians 6:12)

"And I will give unto thee the keys of the kingdom of heaven: and whatsoever thou shalt bind on earth shall be bound in heaven: and whatsoever thou shalt loose on earth shall be loosed in heaven." (Matthew 16:19)

"And he said unto them, I beheld Satan as lightning fall from heaven. Behold, I give unto you power to tread on serpents and scorpions, and over all the power of the enemy: and nothing shall by any means hurt you." (Luke 10:18-19)

I restore the foundations, repair breaches, and build up God ordained walls to keep out the enemies of our souls. I have lived in India and Africa and traveled in Haiti, Southeast Asia and other places where dark spiritual forces are active. In India I once visited the headquarters of the International Society of Krishna Consciousness. I watched people literally prostrate themselves in an attitude of worship to the mostly American and European leaders of the group. As I was taken around I was shown a place where devotees of the Hindu god Krishna and his consort Radha, carried out their daily discipline of chanting and attempting to levitate. In one West African country I was taken to a market where I was told human organs were being sold for juju, which we know as voodoo. In one East African country I visited a city where the streets were strangely without activity. I was told that fear had come on that large city because practitioners of magic had taken people on the street, cut away body parts for spells, and left them bleeding. In another West African country I had more than one close shave out in the countryside with bands of people involved in dark practices and seeking to attack outsiders. America itself also has these kinds of activities to varying degrees, but people tend to seek therapy and medication in America rather than get to the root cause of problems that may have a spiritual origin. People in America and other modern western countries most often do not recognize that the greed, lust, deceit, and hatred, for example, that may be woven into the fabric of their lives may have the involvement of spirits.

A married couple in Africa once came to me and one of my missionary friends to seek our help. The brother of the wife had become so filled with demonic spirits that the couple abandoned their large home to him. When my friend and I arrived on the scene we were met by a wild-eyed young man who then began to tell us in a loud voice with arms flailing that he knew we were coming and perfectly described how we came. I was not impressed. The battle was on. Within the hour the young man was delivered of his tormentors, was in his right mind, and received Jesus as his savior. When I met him some months later at a conference in another part of the country he was still free and growing in his Christian faith.

"Also I heard the voice of the Lord, saying, Whom shall I send, and who will go for us? Then said I, Here am I; send me." (Isaiah 6:8)

"And [they that shall be] of thee shall build the old waste places: thou shalt raise up the foundations of many generations; and thou shalt be called, the repairer of the breach, the restorer of paths to dwell in." (Isaiah 58:12)

"There is a conspiracy of her prophets in the midst thereof, like a roaring lion ravening the prey; they have devoured souls; they have taken the treasure and precious things; they have made her many widows in the midst thereof. Her priests have violated my law, and have profaned mine holy things: they have put no difference between the holy and profane, neither have they shewed difference between the unclean and the clean, and have hid their eyes from my sabbaths, and I am profaned among them. Her princes in the midst thereof are like wolves ravening the prey, to shed blood, and to destroy souls, to get dishonest gain. And her prophets have daubed them with untempered morter, seeing vanity, and divining lies unto them, saying, Thus saith the Lord GOD, when the LORD hath not spoken. The people of the land have used oppression, and exercised robbery, and have vexed the poor

*and needy: yea, they have oppressed the stranger wrongfully.
And I sought for a man among them, that should make up
the hedge, and stand in the gap before me for the land, that I
should not destroy it: but I found none."* (Ezekiel 22:25-30)

*I bring the light of God where there was darkness and deliver many from
the bondage of captivity to life in the light and freedom of the Kingdom of
God.* I step up and do what Jesus Christ commissioned and equipped
His followers to do.

*"And [if] thou draw out thy soul to the hungry, and satisfy
the afflicted soul; then shall thy light rise in obscurity, and thy
darkness [be] as the noonday."* (Isaiah 58:10)

*"To open their eyes, [and] to turn [them] from darkness to
light, and [from] the power of Satan unto God, that they may
receive forgiveness of sins, and inheritance among them which
are sanctified by faith that is in me."* (Acts 26:18)

*"But ye [are] a chosen generation, a royal priesthood, an holy
nation, a peculiar people; that ye should shew forth the praises
of him who hath called you out of darkness into his marvelous
light."* (1 Peter 2:9)

In my life and in the lives of others whose souls have been scared by
others or by our own wrong choices and habits, I, by the Spirit of God,
bring recovery of that which was damaged or stolen, deliverance from
enslavement, and the gifts of restoration, healing, and reconciliation.
Many lives in this world have been damaged to the point that people
despair of ever being helped out of their woeful condition. Just as I have
been brought back into fellowship with Christ, I have been commissioned
to act on behalf of Jesus, as His emissary, to bring others back into relationship with Him.

*"For it shall come to pass in that day, saith the LORD of
hosts, [that] I will break his yoke from off thy neck, and will*

burst thy bonds, and strangers shall no more serve themselves of him." (Jeremiah 30:8)

"And all things [are] of God, who hath reconciled us to himself by Jesus Christ, and hath given to us the ministry of reconciliation; to wit, that God was in Christ, reconciling the world unto himself, not imputing their trespasses unto them; and hath committed unto us the word of reconciliation. Now then we are ambassadors for Christ, as though God did beseech [you] by us: we pray [you] in Christ's stead, be ye reconciled to God." (2 Corinthians 5:18-20)

I am more than a conqueror through Him that loved me. History tells of a King Pyrrhus who was infamous for the high cost of a victory in battle against the Romans. The king is said to have declared that with another such victory they would be lost. Although I am up against tough opposition, Jesus has invested Himself in the certainty of my victory over that opposition. Jesus Christ is my victory and in Him there are no Pyrrhic victories, but rather I am an overwhelming conqueror by Him.

"Nay, in all these things we are more than conquerors through him that loved us." (Romans 8:37)

"And the God of peace shall bruise Satan under your feet shortly. The grace of our Lord Jesus Christ [be] with you. Amen." (Romans 16:20)

You are Yahweh Elohay, the Lord my God who cares for me. God cares for me, not just for a multitude that includes me, but for me and for you individually. He not only cares when we are tempted to think that no one cares, but He is also able and willing to deliver us, as He did when He sent Jesus Christ to die for us in our place.

"Casting all your care upon him; for he careth for you." (1 Peter 5:7)

"And hope maketh not ashamed; because the love of God is shed abroad in our hearts by the Holy Ghost which is given unto us. For when we were yet without strength, in due time Christ died for the ungodly. For scarcely for a righteous man will one die: yet peradventure for a good man some would even dare to die. But God commendeth his love toward us, in that, while we were yet sinners, Christ died for us." (Romans 5:5-8)

"But when he saw the multitudes, he was moved with compassion on them, because they fainted, and were scattered abroad, as sheep having no shepherd." (Matthew 9:36)

"Who comforteth us in all our tribulation, that we may be able to comfort them which are in any trouble, by the comfort wherewith we ourselves are comforted of God. For as the sufferings of Christ abound in us, so our consolation also aboundeth by Christ." (2 Corinthians 1:3-4)

Nothing shall separate me from the love of Christ. The revelation that God has given of His love for me by the plan of salvation that centered on the death of God the Son, Jesus Christ, in my place, has caused a love for God to well up inside me that cannot be broken. My love for God and relationship of fellowship with Him is forever. As many as are willing can know that same love bond.

"Who shall separate us from the love of Christ? [shall] tribulation, or distress, or persecution, or famine, or nakedness, or peril, or sword? As it is written, For thy sake we are killed all the day long; we are accounted as sheep for the slaughter. Nay, in all these things we are more than conquerors through him that loved us. For I am persuaded, that neither death, nor life, nor angels, nor principalities, nor powers, nor things present, nor things to come, Nor height, nor depth, nor any other creature, shall be able to separate us from the love of God, which is in Christ Jesus our Lord." (Romans 8:35-39)

Bold Declarations of Victory

I rule and reign with Christ now, in this time, and in the ages to come. I have the word of Jesus Christ that my hope is not just for the relief of the sweet bye and bye up yonder, but includes ruling in the Kingdom of God, now, in this life, and in the life to come.

> *"And he said unto them, Verily I say unto you, There is no man that hath left house, or parents, or brethren, or wife, or children, for the kingdom of God's sake, who shall not receive manifold more in this present time, and in the world to come life everlasting."* (Luke 18:29-30)

> *"And from Jesus Christ, [who is] the faithful witness, [and] the first begotten of the dead, and the prince of the kings of the earth. Unto him that loved us, and washed us from our sins in his own blood, And hath made us kings and priests unto God and his Father; to him [be] glory and dominion for ever and ever. Amen."* (Revelation 1:5-6)

My enemies are defeated whether they be in the flesh or from the spirit realm. My enemies can give it their best shot, whether they are human or from the spiritual dimension, but they will be defeated.

> *"Now thanks [be] unto God, which always causeth us to triumph in Christ, and maketh manifest the savour of his knowledge by us in every place."* (2 Corinthians 2:14)

> *"No weapon that is formed against thee shall prosper; and every tongue [that] shall rise against thee in judgment thou shalt condemn. This [is] the heritage of the servants of the LORD, and their righteousness [is] of me, saith the LORD."* (Isaiah 54:17)

The devil, his demons, the kingdom of darkness, and the world system are defeated. Jesus Christ died for my sins, went to hell and defeated satan, even before God the Father restored to Him all of the power and glory that He laid aside in order to become a man capable of dying as the sacrificed Lamb of God. That defeat of satan is a fact. I war against the powers of darkness in the knowledge that my Lord has already defeated them.

> *"For we wrestle not against flesh and blood, but against principalities, against powers, against the rulers of the darkness of this world, against spiritual wickedness in high [places]."* (Ephesians 6:12)

> *"And having spoiled principalities and powers, he made a shew of them openly, triumphing over them in it."* (Colossians 2:15)

The power of sin and of condemnation over my life and destiny is broken. I walk in the spirit by the power of the blood of Jesus and of the Spirit. I choose to do so and I reject giving in to the pull of my flesh for ungodly pleasures. Therefore my past record of offenses is wiped clean and no charges of the enemy can stick to me.

> *"[There is] therefore now no condemnation to them which are in Christ Jesus, who walk not after the flesh, but after the Spirit."* (Romans 8:1)

> *"The Spirit of the Lord GOD is upon me; because the LORD hath anointed me to preach good tidings unto the meek; he hath sent me to bind up the brokenhearted, to proclaim liberty to the captives, and the opening of the prison to them that are bound."* (Isaiah 61:1)

In the power and authority of Jesus name I speak to the mountains of debt, diabetes, back problems, and excess weight and command them to go! I speak to my greatest personal challenges commanding them to go. I daily take dominion over more and more territory in those areas. I expect complete victory as I continue.

"And Jesus answering saith unto them, Have faith in God. For verily I say unto you, that whosoever shall say unto this mountain, Be thou removed, and be thou cast into the sea; and shall not doubt in his heart, but shall believe that those things which he saith shall come to pass; he shall have whatsoever he saith. Therefore I say unto you, what things soever ye desire, when ye pray, believe that ye receive [them], and ye shall have [them]." (Mark 11:22-24)

"And whatsoever ye shall ask in my name, that will I do, that the Father may be glorified in the Son. If ye shall ask any thing in my name, I will do it." (John 14:13-14)

Debt is defeated and cancelled. Lack and the spirit of poverty are defeated. The devourer is rebuked. My finances are changed as I stand in the realization of these truths. Just as salvation and cleansing from sin are part of my covenant agreement and provisions from God, so too is victory over the enemy's attempts to impoverish me and laden me with debt.

"But thou shalt remember the LORD thy God: for it is he that giveth thee power to get wealth, that he may establish his covenant which he sware unto thy fathers, as it is this day." (Deuteronomy 8:18)

"Restore, I pray you, to them, even this day, their lands, their vineyards, their oliveyards, and their houses, also the hundredth part of the money, and of the corn, the wine, and the oil, that ye exact of them. Then said they, We will restore them, and will require nothing of them; so will we do as thou sayest. Then I called the priests, and took an oath of them, that they should do according to this promise." (Nehemiah 5:11-12)

"For ye know the grace of our Lord Jesus Christ, that, though he was rich, yet for your sakes he became poor, that ye through his poverty might be rich." (2 Corinthians 8:9)

"And I will rebuke the devourer for your sakes, and he shall not destroy the fruits of your ground; neither shall your vine cast her fruit before the time in the field, saith the LORD of hosts." (Malachi 3:11)

The thief is defeated. Jesus has already defeated satan the thief and causes me to also have victory in my encounters with that same enemy.

"The thief cometh not, but for to steal, and to kill, and to destroy: I am come that they might have life, and that they might have [it] more abundantly." (John 10:10)

"Now thanks be unto God, which always causeth us to triumph in Christ, and maketh manifest the savour of his knowledge by us in every place." (2 Corinthians 2:14)

You are Yahweh Rophe, God my healer, therefore diabetes, obesity, arthritis, allergies, back problems, and all sicknesses are defeated. My healing is of the Lord. As a young pre-teen, I received a miraculous healing from a heart murmur caused by the defect of a hole in my heart. As I stood before God in prayer I felt a warmth come over me and a knowing that I was healed of the heart condition. So the next time I went for my regular checkup I decided that I would not say anything, but see what the doctor would say to confirm my healing. The doctor put his stethoscope on my chest to listen to the heart murmur. That was the usual routine. But this time he could not hear the telltale heart murmur. He called in a second and third doctor. Each of them tried without success to hear the heart murmur that was no longer there. Finally, a fourth doctor came into the examination room. After he said some unflattering things about the skills of the other doctors he pompously rubbed the flat part of his stethoscope, placed it on my chest, and then listened to my heart. To their amazement, they all had to recognize that I no longer had a heart murmur.

I was also suddenly raised up from paralysis from my waist down from an attack of rheumatic fever when I was eight years old. I was in a hospital ward of young boys that included one 14 year old who was crippled with polio. Some of the other younger boys would help to feed him at times because he could do little more than flop his head from side to side and suck in nourishment through a straw. I did not want to share the fate of that boy. Although I was young, I recalled a sermon in which the minister preached about King Hezekiah and how he turned his head to the wall and prayed after being informed of his soon expected death. So in faith one quiet night, under the harsh glare of a naked light bulb from the corridor, I turned my face to the wall and prayed for God to heal me. Then a couple of mornings later I saw my toe move. I then tried to wiggle all of my toes and they moved! I then moved my leg. In no time I was jumping and leaping on my hospital bed with joy. This was so strange that I was taken to the center pit of a dark theater filled with doctors as my strange case was discussed.

In each instance, I looked to God as my healer and He healed me. I approach God my healer for total healing from all other physical issues that have attacked my body. In doing so, I am also mindful to be attentive to the will of God and to walk in His ways by the decision of my will and by the power of Holy Spirit God. God also allows me to carry that healing to others so that they too can be free.

> *"But he [was] wounded for our transgressions, [he was] bruised for our iniquities: the chastisement of our peace [was] upon him; and with his stripes we are healed."* (Isaiah 53:5)

> *"Who his own self bare our sins in his own body on the tree, that we, being dead to sins, should live unto righteousness: by whose stripes ye were healed."* (1 Peter 2:24)

> *"[[A Psalm] of David.] Bless the LORD, O my soul: and all that is within me, [bless] his holy name. Bless the LORD, O my soul, and forget not all his benefits: Who forgiveth all thine iniquities; who healeth all thy diseases."* (Psalm 103:1-3)

> *"And said, If thou wilt diligently hearken to the voice of the LORD thy God, and wilt do that which is right in his sight, and wilt give ear to his commandments, and keep all his*

statutes, I will put none of these diseases upon thee, which I have brought upon the Egyptians: for I am the LORD that healeth thee." (Exodus 15:26)

I bind and take authority over all the power of the enemy in Jesus' name. By faith in the promises of Jesus, I take up and use the authority He has given me as a believer to act as His representative and do the things He did when He walked the earth.

"And I will give unto thee the keys of the kingdom of heaven: and whatsoever thou shalt bind on earth shall be bound in heaven: and whatsoever thou shalt loose on earth shall be loosed in heaven." (Matthew 16:19)

"And the seventy returned again with joy, saying, Lord, even the devils are subject unto us through thy name. And he said unto them, I beheld Satan as lightning fall from heaven. Behold, I give unto you power to tread on serpents and scorpions, and over all the power of the enemy: and nothing shall by any means hurt you." (Luke 10:17-19)

The Restorer and Rewarder

You are Yahweh Gmolah, the Lord of recompense who rewards and compensates Your children. I am compensated in this life and in the life to come by a just and loving God who keeps His promises. He will also see that my unrepentant enemies receive what is the just return for their actions toward me.

"Behold, the righteous shall be recompensed in the earth: much more the wicked and the sinner." (Proverbs 11:31)

"For we know him that hath said, Vengeance [belongeth] unto me, I will recompense, saith the Lord. And again, The Lord shall judge his people." (Hebrews 10:30)

"He withdraweth not his eyes from the righteous: but with kings [are they] on the throne; yea, he doth establish them for ever, and they are exalted." (Job 36:7)

You restore all that has been stolen from me and give me a recompense of double that which was stolen. Your justice, when the thief is caught, restores to me seven times what was stolen. It is the nature of God to restore to me multiples of what the enemy had temporarily taken from me. In faith, I stand expecting recompense from God, and He does not disappoint.

"For your shame [ye shall have] double; and [for] confusion they shall rejoice in their portion: therefore in their land they shall possess the double: everlasting joy shall be unto them." (Isaiah 61:7)

"Turn you to the strong hold, ye prisoners of hope: even to day do I declare [that] I will render double unto thee." (Zechariah 9:12)

"[Men] do not despise a thief, if he steal to satisfy his soul when he is hungry; but [if] he be found, he shall restore sevenfold; he shall give all the substance of his house." (Proverbs 6:30-31)

CHAPTER 8
I HAVE GOD'S FAVOR, BLESSING, PROVISION, AND JOY

I am made the righteousness of God, Yahweh Tsidkenu, in Christ Jesus. My name is written in the Lamb's Book of Life. Increase, favor, and the Blessing are mine. I have access into the manifest presence of God on a spirit to Spirit basis. I boldly ascend and enter into the throne room of the glory to worship God and then receive and bring into my world those revelations and gifts needful to establishing the dominion of God's kingdom on earth. I command a window in heaven to be opened over me through which angels ascend and descend with my heavenly Father's provision for me. I loose my blessings and wealth from the blocking of delaying, hindering spirits and command money and good things to come to me now. Good things: riches, money, favor, grace, wisdom, peace, joy, life, blessings, enriching ideas received and implemented, success, prosperity, God's manifest presence, and His ministering holy angels are all attracted to me. People give me advantages, preferential treatment, favor, money, and beneficial things. The wealth of the wicked and the hidden treasures of darkness are laid up for me. God gives me witty inventions to patent and by which to profit. God takes pleasure in blessing me with wealth to establish His covenant, and I honor Adonai, the Lord my master, with my substance. I have plenty because You are Yahweh Jireh, the Lord my provider who sees my needs and supplies where there was lack. My cup of blessing overflows. I have all that I desire and my joy is full. My Lord is the God of all joy and He bids me to enter into His joy. The joy of the

Lord is my strength. He causes me to laugh with joy because of His salvation, redemption, deliverance, victory, blessing, and His word.

Rightstanding with God

I am made the righteousness of God, Yahweh Tsidkenu, in Christ Jesus. By faith, I appropriate the righteousness of Jesus Christ so that I can be in right standing with God. He makes me have that righteousness. Nothing I can do or have done will suffice; otherwise Jesus didn't have to suffer the death of the cross. So I proclaim my righteousness, not mine really, but the righteousness God makes me to have in Christ Jesus.

Righteousness God makes me to have in Christ Jesus

"For he hath made him [to be] sin for us, who knew no sin; that we might be made the righteousness of God in him." (2 Corinthians 5:21)

"And be found in him, not having mine own righteousness, which is of the law, but that which is through the faith of Christ, the righteousness which is of God by faith." (Philippians 3:9)

"No weapon that is formed against thee shall prosper; and every tongue [that] shall rise against thee in judgment thou shalt condemn. This [is] the heritage of the servants of the LORD, and their righteousness [is] of me, saith the LORD." (Isaiah 54:17)

"Behold, the days come, saith the LORD, that I will raise unto David a righteous Branch, and a King shall reign and prosper, and shall execute judgment and justice in the earth. In his days Judah shall be saved, and Israel shall dwell safely: and this [is] his name whereby he shall be called, THE LORD OUR RIGHTEOUSNESS." (Jeremiah 23:5-6)

My name is written in the Lamb's Book of Life. My name is written down in heaven based on my relationship to the sacrifice of Jesus Christ and His precious blood that was poured out for me. Therefore I have access to the halls of heaven now, in the spirit, and in the life to come when I shall be as He is.

I have access to the halls of heaven now, in the spirit, and in the life to come

"Notwithstanding in this rejoice not, that the spirits are subject unto you; but rather rejoice, because your names are written in heaven." (Luke 10:20)

"And whosoever was not found written in the book of life was cast into the lake of fire." (Revelation 20:15)

Increase, favor, and the Blessing are mine. I seek God and am stirred with love for Him. He will do nothing less than put His blessing on me and grant me His favor.

"And it shall come to pass, if thou shalt hearken diligently unto the voice of the LORD thy God, to observe [and] to do all his commandments which I command thee this day, that the LORD thy God will set thee on high above all nations of the earth: and all these blessings shall come on thee, and overtake thee, if thou shalt hearken unto the voice of the LORD thy God." (Deuteronomy 28:1-2)

"I love them that love me; and those that seek me early shall find me. Riches and honour [are] with me; [yea], durable riches and righteousness. My fruit [is] better than gold, yea, than fine gold; and my revenue than choice silver. I lead in the way of righteousness, in the midst of the paths of judgment: that I may cause those that love me to inherit substance; and I will fill their treasures." (Proverbs 8:17-21)

"The blessing of the LORD, it maketh rich, and he addeth no sorrow with it." (Proverbs 10:22)

"The LORD make his face shine upon thee, and be gracious unto thee." (Numbers 6:25)

"Thou hast granted me life and favour, and thy visitation hath preserved my spirit." (Job 10:12)

Accessing the Presence of God

I have access into the manifest presence of God on a spirit to Spirit basis. It is God's good pleasure for me, in the spirit, to approach Him to worship and experience a relationship of fellowship. This is made possible in the spirit and by Him making me the righteousness of Christ Jesus so that we can have an intimate closeness together in heavenly places. It is a relationship that He wants me to seek in order to take advantage of the way that Jesus has made for me, by His own blood's sacrifice, into the manifest presence of God.

The conversation of Jesus with the Samaritan woman at the well, as recorded in John chapter 4, is remarkable for a statement that Jesus made when the woman tried to make an issue of the difference between Samaritans and Jews regarding where they should go to worship. Jesus explained to her that the time was coming when true worshippers would not worship in Jerusalem. This is astounding given the history of Jerusalem, the city that the Bible many times refers to as the holy city. Jerusalem is the city that the Bible instructed people to go to as they marked holy feasts and offered sacrifices. Jerusalem is the city where the temple was located and was the center of temple worship with its many blood sacrifices and non-stop worship in song as instituted by King David. Jesus taught the words of life in the temple at Jerusalem. Jerusalem is where Jesus spilled his blood in the streets as he carried his cross to his appointed crucifixion to pay the price for the sins of humankind.

For centuries pilgrims, myself included, have gone to Jerusalem, yet Jesus said the time is coming when true worshippers won't worship in

Jerusalem. This raises the question "then where will true worshippers offer the worship in spirit referred to by Jesus?" First of all, that time spoken of by Jesus has not yet come, but when it does it will be a new dispensation of time when the holy Jerusalem spoken of in Revelation chapters 21 and 22 will descend from heaven. It will be near, but not touch or land upon earth. It will not be the physical Jerusalem that we now know, but something new.

This New Jerusalem descending from above will be planetary in its size, but not a physical place. It will not be restricted by the laws of physics as is readily ascertainable from its shape. Other objects of its size in the physical universe tend to be spherical. Unlike earth where its inhabitants dwell on its surface, the redeemed in the New Jerusalem will dwell inside it making it truly the largest city imaginable. Like a bright jewel its light will be seen in both the physical and spiritual dimensions, and the glory of the risen savior Jesus Christ will be the light of that city. Flesh and blood worshippers who are permitted to enter will do so by the spirit and not with their physical bodies. They will ascend to that holy place to offer worship in spirit. That time has not yet come, but God has provided a taste of that time to come through people who have been permitted to ascend to heaven and then descend back to earth. The account in Exodus 24:9-11 describes a group encounter that was a foretaste of that time still to come.

In the meantime, our position as believers and worshippers is that our spirits are already seated in heavenly places with Christ Jesus. In 2 Corinthians 4:7 we are made to know that we already have this treasure, the presence of God, dwelling in our mortal bodies. We can also seek the face of God now and speak with Him in prayer knowing that He hears us and that our great high priest, the Lord Jesus Christ, continually intercedes for us so that we are seen by the Father through the righteousness of Christ. Although it will be great when the new holy city arrives, we don't have to wait for a new dispensation of time to worship God in spirit. In 1 Corinthians 6:20 the apostle Paul instructs us to glorify God in our bodies and spirits, which are God's. He also instructs us in

1 Corinthians 14:15 and in Ephesians 6:18 to pray in the spirit. From the time that Jesus poured out His life's blood in a public execution where He was nailed to a cross until dead and buried, rose again and ascended back to the Father where He had all power and glory restored to Him, until now, we can boldly approach the presence of God without any other sacrifice and without any other human, saint, or angelic intermediary. We can do this now because of the redeeming love sacrifice of Jesus Christ. Now, in this time, Holy Spirit God lives in us and our spirits are in God.

"God [is] a Spirit: and they that worship him must worship [him] in spirit and in truth." (John 4:24)

"Let us therefore come boldly unto the throne of grace, that we may obtain mercy, and find grace to help in time of need." (Hebrews 4:16)

"Having therefore, brethren, boldness to enter into the holiest by the blood of Jesus." (Hebrews 10:19)

"But God, who is rich in mercy, for his great love wherewith he loved us, Even when we were dead in sins, hath quickened us together with Christ, (by grace ye are saved;) And hath raised [us] up together, and made [us] sit together in heavenly [places] in Christ Jesus." (Ephesians 2:4-6)

"If ye then be risen with Christ, seek those things which are above, where Christ sitteth on the right hand of God." (Colossians 3:1)

"After this I looked, and, behold, a door [was] opened in heaven: and the first voice which I heard [was] as it were of a trumpet talking with me; which said, Come up hither, and I will shew thee things which must be hereafter. And immediately I was in the spirit: and, behold, a throne was set in heaven, and [one] sat on the throne." (Revelation 4:1-2"

"And Jacob called the name of the place Peniel: for I have seen God face to face, and my life is preserved." (Genesis 32:30)

"Then went up Moses, and Aaron, Nadab, and Abihu, and seventy of the elders of Israel: and they saw the God of Israel: and [there was] under his feet as it were a paved work of a sapphire stone, and as it were the body of heaven in [his] clearness. And upon the nobles of the children of Israel he laid not his hand: also they saw God, and did eat and drink." (Exodus 24:9-11)

"And the LORD spake unto Moses face to face, as a man speaketh unto his friend." (Exodus 33:11"

"If I ascend up into heaven, thou [art] there: if I make my bed in hell, behold, thou [art there]." (Psalm 139:8)

I enter God's presence

I boldly ascend and enter into the throne room of the glory to worship God and then receive and bring into my world those revelations and gifts needful to establishing the dominion of God's kingdom on earth. I seek God in His glorious presence. Because of the righteousness of Jesus Christ and His blood that is imparted to me, I enter God's presence through the way or door that Jesus made for me. Through this portal into God's glory I receive revelations and answers to prayers and petitions that make the difference in the physical world I inhabit in my flesh and blood body designed for existence in this physical realm. For example, once I went into the glory and, in the spirit, received a new skin for a deathly ill relative whose skin had crusted in a thick and monstrous way. It was over an inch thick in places and reminded one of dried out mudflats by the way it cracked into what seemed like plates. I have never seen that condition before and don't want to see it again. I had this particular experience in the glory after visiting the man in a hospital together with my wife. Then the man's former wife and daughter were amazed at the new soft skin that miraculously formed and that the other skin fell away like scales. Prior to that they were beginning to make arrangements for his imminent death. They wanted to know what I had put on him. I made it clear that what I sprinkled on his diseased body was just a point of contact for the release of our faith, but it was God that did the healing.

I want to make it clear that no one ascends into God's presence at will. I certainly don't. The apostle Paul, when speaking of his experience in 2 Corinthians 12:2-4, may have had up to 14 years pass since he had his last experience of ascending. I ask God, if it pleases Him, to take me up, rather than assuming that I can force myself to ascend. On one occasion, when I expressed my desire to go up and be with Him, He spoke to my heart that I first needed to spend more time with Him on this plane. In other words, in the secret place of worship and praise that all of His children would be wise to spend time in at least daily. Enoch walked with God habitually in a close relationship before he was taken up to glory permanently without having to experience death.

"I was in the Spirit on the Lord's day, and heard behind me a great voice, as of a trumpet, Saying, I am Alpha and Omega, the first and the last: and, What thou seest, write in a book, and send [it] unto the seven churches which are in Asia; unto Ephesus, and unto Smyrna, and unto Pergamos, and unto Thyatira, and unto Sardis, and unto Philadelphia, and unto Laodicea." (Revelation 1:10-11)

"After this I looked, and, behold, a door [was] opened in heaven: and the first voice which I heard [was] as it were of a trumpet talking with me; which said, Come up hither, and I will shew thee things which must be hereafter. And immediately I was in the spirit: and, behold, a throne was set in heaven, and [one] sat on the throne." (Revelation 4:1-2)

"And there came unto me one of the seven angels which had the seven vials full of the seven last plagues, and talked with me, saying, Come hither, I will shew thee the bride, the Lamb's wife. And he carried me away in the spirit to a great and high mountain, and shewed me that great city, the holy

Jerusalem, descending out of heaven from God." (Revelation 21:9-10)

"I knew a man in Christ above fourteen years ago, (whether in the body, I cannot tell; or whether out of the body, I cannot tell: God knoweth;) *such an one caught up to the third heaven. And I knew such a man,* (whether in the body, or out of the body, I cannot tell: God knoweth;) *How that he was caught up into paradise, and heard unspeakable words, which it is not lawful for a man to utter."* (2 Corinthians 12:2-4)

"And Moses took the blood, and sprinkled [it] on the people, and said, Behold the blood of the covenant, which the LORD hath made with you concerning all these words. Then went up Moses, and Aaron, Nadab, and Abihu, and seventy of the elders of Israel: And they saw the God of Israel: and [there was] under his feet as it were a paved work of a sapphire stone, and as it were the body of heaven in [his] clearness." (Exodus 24:8-10)

"Who shall ascend into the hill of the LORD? Or who shall stand in his holy place? He that hath clean hands, and a pure heart; who hath not lifted up his soul unto vanity, nor sworn deceitfully. He shall receive the blessing from the LORD, and righteousness from the God of his salvation. This [is] the generation of them that seek him, that seek thy face, O Jacob. Selah." (Psalm 24:3-6)

"Thou hast ascended on high, thou hast led captivity captive: thou hast received gifts for men; yea, [for] the rebellious also, that the LORD God might dwell [among them]. Blessed [be] the Lord, [who] daily loadeth us [with benefits, even] the God of our salvation. Selah." (Psalm 68:18-19)

"Open to me the gates of righteousness: I will go into them, [and] I will praise the LORD: This gate of the LORD, into which the righteous shall enter." (Psalm 118:19-20)

"If I ascend up into heaven, thou [art] there: if I make my bed in hell, behold, thou [art there]." (Psalm 139:8)

"But unto every one of us is given grace according to the measure of the gift of Christ. Wherefore he saith, when he ascended up on high, he led captivity captive, and gave gifts unto men." (Ephesians 4:7-8)

"Let us therefore come boldly unto the throne of grace, that we may obtain mercy, and find grace to help in time of need." (Hebrews 4:16)

"But my God shall supply all your need according to his riches in glory by Christ Jesus." (Philippians 4:19)

Heavenly Provision

I command a window in heaven to be opened over me through which angels ascend and descend with my heavenly Father's provision for me. Some physicists have theorized about worm holes in the fabric of time and space. God has something far better to bridge the gap between earth and the heaven where He sits on His throne. As Jesus did, I can look toward heaven and have a portal or opening appear in the spirit through which I can receive those things that are needed to bring the rule of the Kingdom of God to the place where God is using me and wants me to do His work to His glory. Angels of God shuttle back and forth to do God's bidding, including things specifically relating to how God choses to assist me as I make myself available as a channel of His blessing and dominion.

As Jesus did, I can look toward heaven

"And he dreamed, and behold a ladder set up on the earth, and the top of it reached to heaven: and behold the angels of God ascending and descending on it. And, behold, the LORD

stood above it, and said, I [am] the LORD God of Abraham thy father, and the God of Isaac: the land whereon thou liest, to thee will I give it, and to thy seed; and thy seed shall be as the dust of the earth, and thou shalt spread abroad to the west, and to the east, and to the north, and to the south: and in thee and in thy seed shall all the families of the earth be blessed. And, behold, I [am] with thee, and will keep thee in all [places] whither thou goest, and will bring thee again into this land; for I will not leave thee, until I have done [that] which I have spoken to thee of. And Jacob awaked out of his sleep, and he said, Surely the LORD is in this place; and I knew [it] not. And he was afraid, and said, How dreadful [is] this place! this [is] none other but the house of God, and this [is] the gate of heaven." (Genesis 28:12-17)

"Now it came to pass in the thirtieth year, in the fourth [month], in the fifth [day] of the month, as I [was] among the captives by the river of Chebar, [that] the heavens were opened, and I saw visions of God." (Ezekiel 1:1)

"And he saith unto him, Verily, verily, I say unto you, hereafter ye shall see heaven open, and the angels of God ascending and descending upon the Son of man." (John 1:51)

"And looking up to heaven, he sighed, and saith unto him, Ephphatha, that is, Be opened." (Mark 7:34)

"Then he took the five loaves and the two fishes, and looking up to heaven, he blessed them, and brake, and gave to the disciples to set before the multitude." (Luke 9:16)

"But he, being full of the Holy Ghost, looked up stedfastly into heaven, and saw the glory of God, and Jesus standing on the right hand of God, and said, Behold, I see the heavens opened, and the Son of man standing on the right hand of God." (Acts 7:55-56)

"And Jesus, when he was baptized, went up straightway out of the water: and, lo, the heavens were opened unto him, and he saw the Spirit of God descending like a dove, and lighting upon him: and lo a voice from heaven, saying, This is my beloved Son, in whom I am well pleased." (Matthew 3:16-17)

Taking Possession of My Benefits in Christ

I loose my blessings and wealth from the blocking of delaying, hindering spirits and command money and good things to come to me now. Yes, I have a mansion prepared for me in heaven where the streets are of the purest gold, but I also have blessings and wealth available for use now. There are forces in the spirit world arrayed against me to block or delay my blessings. However, I am not ignorant of them and I take them on directly so that the good things God has appointed for me in this life are received now.

"For the vision [is] yet for an appointed time, but at the end it shall speak, and not lie: though it tarry, wait for it; because it will surely come, it will not tarry." (Habakkuk 2:3)

"For I [am] the LORD: I will speak, and the word that I shall speak shall come to pass; it shall be no more prolonged: for in your days, O rebellious house, will I say the word, and will perform it, saith the Lord GOD." Ezekiel 12:25)

"Then Peter said, Lo, we have left all, and followed thee. And he said unto them, Verily I say unto you, There is no man that hath left house, or parents, or brethren, or wife, or children, for the kingdom of God's sake, who shall not receive manifold more in this present time, and in the world to come life everlasting." (Luke 18:28-30)

"And I will restore to you the years that the locust hath eaten, the cankerworm, and the caterpiller, and the palmerworm, my great army which I sent among you." (Joel 2:25)

"Wherefore we would have come unto you, even I Paul, once and again; but Satan hindered us." (1 Thessalonians 2:18)

"And, behold, an hand touched me, which set me upon my knees and [upon] the palms of my hands. And he said unto me, O Daniel, a man greatly beloved, understand the words that I speak unto thee, and stand upright: for unto thee am I now sent. And when he had spoken this word unto me, I stood trembling. Then said he unto me, Fear not, Daniel: for from the first day that thou didst set thine heart to understand, and to chasten thyself before thy God, thy words were heard, and I am come for thy words. But the prince of the kingdom of Persia withstood me one and twenty days: but, lo, Michael, one of the chief princes, came to help me; and I remained there with the kings of Persia." (Daniel 10:10-13)

"And it shall come to pass in that day, [that] his burden shall be taken away from off thy shoulder, and his yoke from off thy neck, and the yoke shall be destroyed because of the anointing." (Isaiah 10:27)

"This [is] the day [which] the LORD hath made; we will rejoice and be glad in it. Save now, I beseech thee, O LORD: O LORD, I beseech thee, send now prosperity." (Psalm 118:24-25)

Good things: riches, money, favor, grace, wisdom, peace, joy, life, blessings, enriching ideas received and implemented, success, prosperity, God's manifest presence, and His ministering holy angels are all attracted to me. Good things are attracted to me or come to me as a result of me fulfilling my part of the exchange in God's covenant. They come as surely as night follows day. It is not magic. It is not me commandeering angels into my service to do my will. It is not me forcing God to do anything. It is a matter of me aligning myself with the promises of God and then, in faith, expecting God's promises to be fulfilled. Some promises are conditional "if—then" propositions where actions bring a promised reaction or harvest. If I do what God requires then He will surely honor His word of promise, if I look for it in faith, for without faith and ready obedience it is not possible to please God.

Good things are attracted to me

"And it shall come to pass, if thou shalt hearken diligently unto the voice of the LORD thy God, to observe [and] to do all his commandments which I command thee this day, that the LORD thy God will set thee on high above all nations of the earth: and all these blessings shall come on thee, and over- take thee, if thou shalt hearken unto the voice of the LORD thy God." (Deuteronomy 28:1-2)

"Keep therefore the words of this covenant, and do them, that ye may prosper in all that ye do." (Deuteronomy 29:9)

"Are they not all ministering spirits, sent forth to minister for them who shall be heirs of salvation?" (Hebrews 1:14)

"Bring ye all the tithes into the storehouse, that there may be meat in mine house, and prove me now herewith, saith the LORD of hosts, if I will not open you the windows of heaven, and pour you out a blessing, that [there shall] not [be room] enough [to receive it]." (Malachi 3:10)

"This book of the law shall not depart out of thy mouth; but thou shalt meditate therein day and night, that thou mayest observe to do according to all that is written therein: for then thou shalt make thy way prosperous, and then thou shalt have good success." (Joshua 1:8)

"The fear of the wicked, it shall come upon him: but the desire of the righteous shall be granted." (Proverbs 10:24)

"I love them that love me; and those that seek me early shall find me. Riches and honour [are] with me; [yea], durable riches and righteousness. My fruit [is] better than gold, yea,

than fine gold; and my revenue than choice silver. I lead in the way of righteousness, in the midst of the paths of judgment: that I may cause those that love me to inherit substance; and I will fill their treasures." (Proverbs 8:17-21)

"By humility [and] the fear of the LORD [are] riches, and honour, and life." (Proverbs 22:4)

"For the LORD God [is] a sun and shield: the LORD will give grace and glory: no good [thing] will he withhold from them that walk uprightly." (Psalm 84:11)

"Surely goodness and mercy shall follow me all the days of my life: and I will dwell in the house of the LORD for ever." (Psalm 23:6)

"The secret of the LORD [is] with them that fear him; and he will shew them his covenant. Mine eyes [are] ever toward the LORD; for he shall pluck my feet out of the net." (Psalm 25:14-15)

"The angel of the LORD encampeth round about them that fear him, and delivereth them." (Psalm 34:7)

"Let thy tender mercies come unto me, that I may live: for thy law [is] my delight. Let the proud be ashamed; for they dealt perversely with me without a cause: [but] I will meditate in thy precepts." (Psalm 119:77-78)

"[A Song of degrees of David.] Behold, how good and how pleasant [it is] for brethren to dwell together in unity! [It is] like the precious ointment upon the head, that ran down upon the beard, [even] Aaron's beard: that went down to the skirts of his garments; as the dew of Hermon, [and as the dew] that descended upon the mountains of Zion: for there the LORD commanded the blessing, [even] life for evermore." (Psalm 133:1-3)

People give me advantages, preferential treatment, favor, money, and beneficial things. I expect favor and good things, and they come to me.

> *"O Lord, I beseech thee, let now thine ear be attentive to the prayer of thy servant, and to the prayer of thy servants, who desire to fear thy name: and prosper, I pray thee, thy servant this day, and grant him mercy in the sight of this man. For I was the king's cupbearer."* (Nehemiah 1:11)

> *"And Jesus increased in wisdom and stature, and in favour with God and man."* (Luke 2:52)

> *"Give, and it shall be given unto you; good measure, pressed down, and shaken together, and running over, shall men give into your bosom. For with the same measure that ye mete withal it shall be measured to you again."* (Luke 6:38)

The wealth of the wicked and the hidden treasures of darkness are laid up for me. I don't have to strive to come into wealth. It is God's good pleasure to transfer it to me so that I am resourced to give it back into the Kingdom of God.

> *"I will go before thee, and make the crooked places straight: I will break in pieces the gates of brass, and cut in sunder the bars of iron: and I will give thee the treasures of darkness, and hidden riches of secret places, that thou mayest know that I, the LORD, which call [thee] by thy name, [am] the God of Israel."* (Isaiah 45:2-3)

> *"For [God] giveth to a man that [is] good in his sight wisdom, and knowledge, and joy: but to the sinner he giveth travail, to gather and to heap up, that he may give to [him that is] good before God. This also [is] vanity and vexation of spirit."* (Ecclesiastes 2:26)

> *"A good [man] leaveth an inheritance to his children's children: and the wealth of the sinner [is] laid up for the just."* (Proverbs 13:22)

"This [is] the portion of a wicked man with God, and the heritage of oppressors, [which] they shall receive of the Almighty. If his children be multiplied, [it is] for the sword: and his offspring shall not be satisfied with bread. Those that remain of him shall be buried in death: and his widows shall not weep. Though he heap up silver as the dust, and prepare raiment as the clay; he may prepare [it], but the just shall put [it] on, and the innocent shall divide the silver." (Job 27:13-17)

God gives me witty inventions to patent and by which to profit. One idea developed and brought to market can provide wealth for a lifetime. Great scientists like Sir Isaac Newton and Johannes Kepler honored God for their discoveries. God will reveal secrets to me because He can trust me to honor Him.

"I wisdom dwell with prudence, and find out knowledge of witty inventions." (Proverbs 8:12)

"It is the glory of God to conceal a thing: but the honour of kings is to search out a matter." (Proverbs 25:2)

"But thou shalt remember the LORD thy God: for [it is] he that giveth thee power to get wealth, that he may establish his covenant which he sware unto thy fathers, as [it is] this day." (Deuteronomy 8:18)

God takes pleasure in blessing me with wealth to establish His covenant, and I honor Adonai, the Lord my master, with my substance. I grew up as a poor kid who knew hunger and had times of living on welfare and government surplus food like powdered eggs and processed cheese. Moreover, as a member of a minority, I didn't have great advantages, but rather barriers to success in life. Yet, God blessed me and still is blessing me. It is my joy to give back to the Kingdom of God.

"Let them shout for joy, and be glad, that favour my righteous cause: yea, let them say continually, Let the LORD

be magnified, which hath pleasure in the prosperity of his servant." (Psalm 35:27)

"Beloved, I wish above all things that thou mayest prosper and be in health, even as thy soul prospereth." (3 John 1:2)

"Acquaint now thyself with him, and be at peace: thereby good shall come unto thee. Receive, I pray thee, the law from his mouth, and lay up his words in thine heart. If thou return to the Almighty, thou shalt be built up, thou shalt put away iniquity far from thy tabernacles. Then shalt thou lay up gold as dust, and the [gold] of Ophir as the stones of the brooks. Yea, the Almighty shall be thy defence, and thou shalt have plenty of silver. For then shalt thou have thy delight in the Almighty, and shalt lift up thy face unto God. Thou shalt make thy prayer unto him, and he shall hear thee, and thou shalt pay thy vows. Thou shalt also decree a thing, and it shall be established unto thee: and the light shall shine upon thy ways." (Job 22:21-28)

"If they obey and serve [him], they shall spend their days in prosperity, and their years in pleasures." (Job 36:11)

"Praise ye the LORD. Blessed [is] the man [that] feareth the LORD, [that] delighteth greatly in his commandments. His seed shall be mighty upon earth: the generation of the upright shall be blessed. Wealth and riches [shall be] in his house: and his righteousness endureth for ever." (Psalm 112:1-3)

"I love them that love me; and those that seek me early shall find me. Riches and honour [are] with me; [yea], durable riches and righteousness. My fruit [is] better than gold, yea, than fine gold; and my revenue than choice silver. I lead in the way of righteousness, in the midst of the paths of judgment: that I may cause those that love me to inherit substance; and I will fill their treasures." (Proverbs 8:17-21)

"Fear not, little flock; for it is your Father's good pleasure to give you the kingdom." (Luke 12:32)

"Honour the LORD with thy substance, and with the first-fruits of all thine increase." (Proverbs 3:9)

I have plenty because You are Yahweh Jireh, the Lord my provider who sees my needs and supplies where there was lack. God responds to my faith in Him and His nature. For those who believe in Him and His promises there is no lack.

"And Abraham called the name of that place Jehovahjireh: as it is said to this day, In the mount of the LORD it shall be seen." (Genesis 22:14)

"And he said unto them, When I sent you without purse, and scrip, and shoes, lacked ye any thing? And they said, Nothing." (Luke 22:35)

My cup of blessing overflows. God blesses me with the increase of overflow so that I might be a blessing to others to His glory.

"Thou preparest a table before me in the presence of mine enemies: thou anointest my head with oil; my cup runneth over. Surely goodness and mercy shall follow me all the days of my life: and I will dwell in the house of the LORD for ever." (Psalm 23:5-6)

"Blessed [be] the Lord, [who] daily loadeth us [with benefits, even] the God of our salvation. Selah." (Psalm 68:19)

"Thou shalt increase my greatness, and comfort me on every side." (Psalm 71:21)

Living in the Joy

I have all that I desire and my joy is full. My Lord is the God of all joy and He bids me to enter into His joy. The joy of the Lord is my strength. I have great joy in knowing and following the Lord. The joy of His presence is better than all of the pleasures that the world has to offer without God. God is my loving Father and He dotes on all of His children. He is pleased when His children are full of His joy and have His peace.

"The fear of the wicked, it shall come upon him: but the desire of the righteous shall be granted." (Proverbs 10:24)

"Delight thyself also in the LORD; and he shall give thee the desires of thine heart." (Psalm 34:7)

"Thou wilt shew me the path of life: in thy presence [is] fulness of joy; at thy right hand [there are] pleasures for evermore." (Psalm 16:11)

"Then will I go unto the altar of God, unto God my exceeding joy: yea, upon the harp will I praise thee, O God my God." (Psalm 43:4)

"I will greatly rejoice in the LORD, my soul shall be joyful in my God; for he hath clothed me with the garments of salvation, he hath covered me with the robe of righteousness, as a bridegroom decketh [himself] with ornaments, and as a bride adorneth [herself] with her jewels." (Isaiah 61:10)

"Thy words were found, and I did eat them; and thy word was unto me the joy and rejoicing of mine heart: for I am called by thy name, O LORD God of hosts." (Jeremiah 15:16)

"His lord said unto him, Well done, [thou] good and faithful servant: thou hast been faithful over a few things, I will make thee ruler over many things: enter thou into the joy of thy lord." (Matthew 25:21)

"Behold [that] which I have seen: [it is] good and comely [for one] to eat and to drink, and to enjoy the good of all his labour that he taketh under the sun all the days of his life, which God giveth him: for it [is] his portion. Every man also

to whom God hath given riches and wealth, and hath given him power to eat thereof, and to take his portion, and to rejoice in his labour; this [is] the gift of God. For he shall not much remember the days of his life; because God answereth [him] in the joy of his heart." (Ecclesiastes 5:18-20)

"Rejoice evermore." (1 Thessalonians 5:16)

"Rejoice in the Lord alway: [and] again I say, Rejoice." (Philippians 4:4)

"Now the God of hope fill you with all joy and peace in believing, that ye may abound in hope, through the power of the Holy Ghost." (Romans 15:13)

"Serve the LORD with gladness: come before his presence with singing." (Psalm 100:2)

"And now come I to thee; and these things I speak in the world, that they might have my joy fulfilled in themselves." (John 17:13)

"Then he said unto them, Go your way, eat the fat, and drink the sweet, and send portions unto them for whom nothing is prepared: for [this] day [is] holy unto our Lord: neither be ye sorry; for the joy of the LORD is your strength." (Nehemiah 8:10)

He causes me to laugh with joy because of His salvation, redemption, deliverance, victory, blessing, and His word. God is not a stern judge just looking for an excuse to punish me and have me cry in torment. He is instead the life of the party and fills my spirit to overflowing with joy and laughter because of the great things He has done for me.

"And Sarah said, God hath made me to laugh, [so that] all that hear will laugh with me." (Genesis 21:6)

"For the kingdom of God is not meat and drink; but righteousness, and peace, and joy in the Holy Ghost." (Romans 14:17)

"The thief cometh not, but for to steal, and to kill, and to destroy: I am come that they might have life, and that they might have [it] more abundantly." (John 10:10)

"These things have I spoken unto you, that my joy might remain in you, and [that] your joy might be full." (John 15:11)

"But I have trusted in thy mercy; my heart shall rejoice in thy salvation. I will sing unto the LORD, because he hath dealt bountifully with me." (Psalm 13:5-6)

"How excellent [is] thy lovingkindness, O God! therefore the children of men put their trust under the shadow of thy wings. They shall be abundantly satisfied with the fatness of thy house; and thou shalt make them drink of the river of thy pleasures. For with thee [is] the fountain of life: in thy light shall we see light." (Psalm 36:7-9)

"But let the righteous be glad; let them rejoice before God: yea, let them exceedingly rejoice." (Psalm 68:3)

"[A Song of degrees.] When the LORD turned again the captivity of Zion, we were like them that dream. Then was our mouth filled with laughter, and our tongue with singing: then said they among the heathen, The LORD hath done great things for them. The LORD hath done great things for us; [whereof] we are glad. Turn again our captivity, O LORD, as the streams in the south. They that sow in tears shall reap in joy. He that goeth forth and weepeth, bearing precious seed, shall doubtless come again with rejoicing, bringing his sheaves [with him]." (Psalm 126:1-6)

"Till he fill thy mouth with laughing, and thy lips with rejoicing." (Job 8:21)

"Therefore with joy shall ye draw water out of the wells of salvation." (Isaiah 12:3)

"And the ransomed of the LORD shall return, and come to Zion with songs and everlasting joy upon their heads: they shall obtain joy and gladness, and sorrow and sighing shall flee away." (Isaiah 35:10)

"We will rejoice in thy salvation, and in the name of our God we will set up [our] banners: the LORD fulfill all thy petitions." (Psalm 20:5)

CHAPTER 9
I LIVE OUT THE PURPOSE
OF BLESSING AND
EQUIPPING IN MY LIFE

I go about doing good and operate in the gifts of the anointing. I excel in the grace of giving, giving at the level I conceive and determine in my heart. I establish and extend the Kingdom of God wherever I go. I lift up and proclaim the name of Jesus; the God who humbled Himself, came down from heaven in the likeness and limitations of man by a virgin birth as a helpless baby, was crucified in the flesh in payment for the sins of the world, and is risen from the dead, so that men are drawn to Him and are saved. By Him I bear much fruit and it is fruit that remains.

Blessed to be a Blessing

I go about doing good and operate in the gifts of the anointing. Jesus calls on me to replicate His pattern of doing good in the power of the Spirit. I was created to do good works that glorify God. So I look for opportunities to do good and am open to God's leading, being ready to respond.

Created to do good

"But the manifestation of the Spirit is given to every man to profit withal." (1 Corinthians 12:7)

"And [his] brightness was as the light; he had horns [coming] out of his hand: and there [was] the hiding of his power." (Habakkuk 3:4)

"For we are his workmanship, created in Christ Jesus unto good works, which God hath before ordained that we should walk in them." (Ephesians 2:10)

I excel in the grace of giving, giving at the level I conceive and determine in my heart. It is my joy to give into the Kingdom of God. Last year my wife and I counted up what we had given to our church and to Christian ministries since we have been married. It was a pleasant surprise. I see myself doing much greater things in the grace of giving knowing that God will supply the resources necessary to fulfill my heart's desire in this area.

"Therefore, as ye abound in every [thing, in] faith, and utterance, and knowledge, and [in] all diligence, and [in] your love to us, [see] that ye abound in this grace also." (2 Corinthians 8:7)

"Every man according as he purposeth in his heart, [so let him give]; not grudgingly, or of necessity: for God loveth a cheerful giver." (2 Corinthians 9:7)

"I have shewed you all things, how that so labouring ye ought to support the weak, and to remember the words of the Lord Jesus, how he said, It is more blessed to give than to receive." (Acts 20:35)

I establish and extend the Kingdom of God wherever I go. God has commissioned me to take His kingdom wherever I go, and that is a calling I delight to move in.

"And heal the sick that are therein, and say unto them, The kingdom of God is come nigh unto you." (Luke 10:9)

I lift up and proclaim the name of Jesus; very God who humbled Himself, came down from heaven in the likeness and limitations of man by a virgin birth as a helpless baby, was crucified in the flesh in payment for the sins of the world, and is risen from the dead, so that men are drawn to Him and are saved. God has chosen men to be the vehicle to reach other men. Because He became a man, Jesus can and does call His own number and intervenes in the lives of people by appearing to them. This is what He did when He manifested Himself to Saul the persecutor on the road to Damascus to forever change the man God selected to be Paul, a chosen instrument. However, He has also given me a part in that ministry and I joyfully present His amazing story and truth by word and deed.

> *"For unto us a child is born, unto us a son is given: and the government shall be upon his shoulder: and his name shall be called Wonderful, Counsellor, The mighty God, The everlasting Father, The Prince of Peace."* (Isaiah 9:6)

> *"But he [was] wounded for our transgressions, [he was] bruised for our iniquities: the chastisement of our peace [was] upon him; and with his stripes we are healed. All we like sheep have gone astray; we have turned every one to his own way; and the LORD hath laid on him the iniquity of us all."* (Isaiah 53:5-6)

> *"The next day John seeth Jesus coming unto him, and saith, Behold the Lamb of God, which taketh away the sin of the world."* (John 1:29)

> *"Let this mind be in you, which was also in Christ Jesus: who, being in the form of God, thought it not robbery to be equal with God: but made himself of no reputation, and took upon him the form of a servant, and was made in the likeness of men: and being found in fashion as a man, he humbled himself, and became obedient unto death, even the death of the cross. Wherefore God also hath highly exalted him, and given him a name which is above every name: that at the name of Jesus every knee should bow, of [things] in heaven,*

and [things] in earth, and [things] under the earth; and [that]
every tongue should confess that Jesus Christ [is] Lord, to the
glory of God the Father." (Philippians 2:5-11)

By Him I bear much fruit and it is fruit that remains. God thinks
big and does things big. He intends for me to be fruitful through my
attachment to Him and He ensures that the fruit of righteousness that I
produce by His Spirit remains and, in turn, reproduces itself.

"Ye have not chosen me, but I have chosen you, and ordained
you, that ye should go and bring forth fruit, and that your
fruit should remain: that whatsoever ye shall ask of the Father
in my name, he may give it you." (John 15:16)

CHAPTER 10
I AM A SOWER WHO IMITATES GOD

I am a blessing to others to the glory of God. I am generous and I abound to every good work as I am led by the Spirit of Yahweh Rohi, God my shepherd. Almighty God my satisfier and supplier, El Shaddai, gives me seed to sow and multiplies my seed sown. I sow into good soil and reap a hundredfold return. I sow many types of good seed and receive the sure harvests of my expectations and the assignments of those seeds. I nurture the fatherless. I give and keep giving to the poor, widows, and orphans, and God blesses me all the more.

Going About Imitating Christ

I am a blessing to others to the glory of God. I do what God put me here to do, and that is to do the works of God and lead others into a relationship with Him through faith in Jesus Christ.

> *"Let your light so shine before men, that they may see your good works, and glorify your Father which is in heaven."*
> (Matthew 5:16)

I am generous and I abound to every good work as I am led by the Spirit of Yahweh Rohi, God my shepherd. I don't lack, nor do I have just barely enough, rather I have abundant resources from which I bless others in response to the leading of God.

"[A Psalm of David.] The LORD [is] my shepherd; I shall not want." (Psalm 23:1)

"Howbeit when he, the Spirit of truth, is come, he will guide you into all truth: for he shall not speak of himself; but whatsoever he shall hear, [that] shall he speak: and he will shew you things to come." (John 16:13)

"That they do good, that they be rich in good works, ready to distribute, willing to communicate." (1 Timothy 6:18)

Almighty God my satisfier and supplier, El Shaddai, gives me seed to sow and multiplies my seed sown. I give even as God is a giver, and I ask for and receive more seed to sow so that I can continue to give and show that I am truly His son.

"And God [is] able to make all grace abound toward you; that ye, always having all sufficiency in all [things], may abound to every good work: (As it is written, He hath dispersed abroad; he hath given to the poor: his righteousness remaineth for ever. Now he that ministereth seed to the sower both minister bread for [your] food, and multiply your seed sown, and increase the fruits of your righteousness;) *being enriched in every thing to all bountifulness, which causeth through us thanksgiving to God."* (2 Corinthians 9:8-11)

I sow into good soil and reap a hundredfold return. I sow many types of good seed and receive the sure harvests of my expectations and the assignments of those seeds. I expect a good return on everything that I sow be it time, prayers, money, gifts, counseling, encouragement, words of faith, or any other thing that God leads me to do.

"Then Isaac sowed in that land, and received in the same year an hundredfold: and the LORD blessed him." (Genesis 26:12)

"And Jesus answered and said, Verily I say unto you, There is no man that hath left house, or brethren, or sisters, or father, or mother, or wife, or children, or lands, for my sake, and the gospel's, But he shall receive an hundredfold now in this time, houses, and brethren, and sisters, and mothers, and children, and lands, with persecutions; and in the world to come eternal life." (Mark 10:29-30)

"Give, and it shall be given unto you; good measure, pressed down, and shaken together, and running over, shall men give into your bosom. For with the same measure that ye mete withal it shall be measured to you again." (Luke 6:38)

The Least of These

I nurture the fatherless. I give and keep giving to the poor, widows, and orphans, and God blesses me all the more. This can be a tough world. It is even more so to the fatherless, orphans, the poverty stricken, and widows, especially in cultures where women are not valued in the first place. Part of my charge from God is to be His hand extended to those who cry out to Him for help. When I lived in Calcutta, India it was my privilege to know a long time missionary couple who founded a great mission. These two precious people arrived there decades earlier with little, but responded to the tangible physical needs of the people they ministered to at the same time as they fed their spiritual needs for life in Christ Jesus. Over time, thousands of people were being fed daily, orphanages set up, schools, churches, and a hospital that was one of the best in Calcutta and that did many pro bono procedures. They also set up a nursing school that turned out that huge nation's top nurses based on objective competitive examination results. Many other good things they did while choosing to live modestly. What an example! God has also placed in my heart the desire to do similar things for His glory and to respond to the needs of the least among us.

Be His hand extended

"Pure religion and undefiled before God and the Father is this, To visit the fatherless and widows in their affliction, [and] to keep himself unspotted from the world." (James 1:27)

"And the King shall answer and say unto them, Verily I say unto you, Inasmuch as ye have done [it] unto one of the least of these my brethren, ye have done [it] unto me." (Matthew 25:40)

"Defend the poor and fatherless: do justice to the afflicted and needy." (Psalm 82:3)

Chapter 11

I Demonstrate the Power of the Spoken Word of Faith in Partnership with Holy Spirit God

I guard my heart and my mouth. I do not sin with my words. I speak life. My spoken words contain and release the power of my faith in the immutable promises of God. The sword of the Spirit is a powerful weapon wielded by my mouth. By the Spirit of Christ and the Word spoken in faith, I deliver and set captives free, break chains that bind, remit the sins of those who have sinned against me, and undo heavy burdens. I pull down strongholds. The gates of hell and its counsels shall not prevail. As God's ambassador and a citizen of the Kingdom of God, Elohim, God the creator's Word in my mouth is as powerful as His Word spoken by His mouth. So shall my word be that goes forth out of my mouth; it shall accomplish that which I please and shall be successful in the matter to which I assign it. I request of God my Father and He dispatches ministering spirits. They are more and stronger that be with me than those that come against me and the Kingdom of God. The holy angels of God minister to me. They harken to the voice of God's Word that I speak with faith, and God directs them to perform it. I believe that I receive. Life is in the power of my tongue. I love it and eat the fruit of it. I have what I say. I see it with the eye of faith and the images I conceive and meditate upon in my thoughts are established and manifested in this realm as in heaven. I agree with the Word of God. I obtain the promises of God.

The Power of Words and the Heart-Mouth Connection

I guard my heart and my mouth. I do not sin with my words. I speak life. I check myself frequently to ensure that what comes out of my mouth is intentional and what I want to see come about. I remind myself to speak into existence those end states that have not yet appeared. It has not always been that way. Some years ago in the midst of a powerful encounter with God, I plainly heard His voice audibly saying to me "My son, can sweet water and bitter come from the same well?" That was quite a rebuke. It got my attention to lift my words to a higher level and not cause pain to others with my sharp tongue and thoughtless, inconsiderate, stinging wit.

> *"Keep thy heart with all diligence; for out of it [are] the issues of life."* (Proverbs 4:23)

> *"For he that will love life, and see good days, let him refrain his tongue from evil, and his lips that they speak no guile."* (1 Peter 3:10)

> *"Let the words of my mouth, and the meditation of my heart, be acceptable in thy sight, O LORD, my strength, and my redeemer."* (Psalm 19:14)

> *"[To the chief Musician, [even] to Jeduthun, A Psalm of David.] I said, I will take heed to my ways, that I sin not with my tongue: I will keep my mouth with a bridle, while the wicked is before me."* (Psalm 39:1)

> *"For in many things we offend all. If any man offend not in word, the same [is] a perfect man, [and] able also to bridle the whole body. Behold, we put bits in the horses' mouths, that they may obey us; and we turn about their whole body. Behold also the ships, which though [they be] so great, and [are] driven of fierce winds, yet are they turned about with a very small helm, whithersoever the governor listeth. Even*

so the tongue is a little member, and boasteth great things. Behold, how great a matter a little fire kindleth! And the tongue [is] a fire, a world of iniquity: so is the tongue among our members, that it defileth the whole body, and setteth on fire the course of nature; and it is set on fire of hell. For every kind of beasts, and of birds, and of serpents, and of things in the sea, is tamed, and hath been tamed of mankind: But the tongue can no man tame; [it is] an unruly evil, full of deadly poison. Therewith bless we God, even the Father; and therewith curse we men, which are made after the similitude of God. Out of the same mouth proceedeth blessing and cursing. My brethren, these things ought not so to be. Doth a fountain send forth at the same place sweet [water] and bitter? Can the fig tree, my brethren, bear olive berries? Either a vine, figs? So [can] no fountain both yield salt water and fresh.” (James 3:2-12)

“Either make the tree good, and his fruit good; or else make the tree corrupt, and his fruit corrupt: for the tree is known by [his] fruit. O generation of vipers, how can ye, being evil, speak good things? For out of the abundance of the heart the mouth speaketh. A good man out of the good treasure of the heart bringeth forth good things: and an evil man out of the evil treasure bringeth forth evil things. But I say unto you, that every idle word that men shall speak, they shall give account thereof in the day of judgment. For by thy words thou shalt be justified, and by thy words thou shalt be condemned.” (Matthew 12:33-37)

“Death and life [are] in the power of the tongue: and they that love it shall eat the fruit thereof.” (Proverbs 18:21)

My spoken words contain and release the power of my faith in the immutable promises of God. When I face a challenge I speak out the word of God and remind God my Father that He cannot lie and that no one can make Him into a liar by altering my circumstances in such a way that it would nullify the promises of God.

"Wherein God, willing more abundantly to shew unto the heirs of promise the immutability of his counsel, confirmed [it] by an oath: that by two immutable things, in which [it was] impossible for God to lie, we might have a strong consolation, who have fled for refuge to lay hold upon the hope set before us." (Hebrews 6:17-18)

"And Jesus answering saith unto them, Have faith in God. For verily I say unto you, that whosoever shall say unto this mountain, Be thou removed, and be thou cast into the sea; and shall not doubt in his heart, but shall believe that those things which he saith shall come to pass; he shall have whatsoever he saith. Therefore I say unto you, what things soever ye desire, when ye pray, believe that ye receive [them], and ye shall have [them]." (Mark 11:22-24)

"So shall my word be that goeth forth out of my mouth: it shall not return unto me void, but it shall accomplish that which I please, and it shall prosper [in the thing] whereto I sent it." (Isaiah 55:11)

"He staggered not at the promise of God through unbelief; but was strong in faith, giving glory to God; And being fully persuaded that, what he had promised, he was able also to perform." (Romans 4:20-21)

"For all the promises of God in him [are] yea, and in him Amen, unto the glory of God by us." (2 Corinthians 1:20)

"In hope of eternal life, which God, that cannot lie, promised before the world began." (Titus 1:2)

There is a Sharp Sword in My Mouth

The sword of the Spirit is a powerful weapon wielded by my mouth. Spirit words are weapons and I speak them out loud from my mouth expecting them to accomplish the things I have uttered them for because I am confident I have the authority to do so.

Spirit words are weapons

"Finally, my brethren, be strong in the Lord, and in the power of his might. Put on the whole armour of God, that ye may be able to stand against the wiles of the devil. For we wrestle not against flesh and blood, but against principalities, against powers, against the rulers of the darkness of this world, against spiritual wickedness in high [places]. Wherefore take unto you the whole armour of God, that ye may be able to withstand in the evil day, and having done all, to stand. Stand therefore, having your loins girt about with truth, and having on the breastplate of righteousness; and your feet shod with the preparation of the gospel of peace; above all, taking the shield of faith, wherewith ye shall be able to quench all the fiery darts of the wicked. And take the helmet of salvation, and the sword of the Spirit, which is the word of God: praying always with all prayer and supplication in the Spirit, and watching thereunto with all perseverance and supplication for all saints." (Ephesians 6:10-18)

"For the word of God [is] quick, and powerful, and sharper than any twoedged sword, piercing even to the dividing asunder of soul and spirit, and of the joints and marrow, and [is] a discerner of the thoughts and intents of the heart." (Hebrews 4:12)

And he hath made my mouth like a sharp sword; in the shadow of his hand hath he hid me, and made me a polished shaft; in his quiver hath he hid me." (Isaiah 49:2)

"And he had in his right hand seven stars: and out of his mouth went a sharp twoedged sword: and his countenance [was] as the sun shineth in his strength." (Revelation 1:16)

"Repent; or else I will come unto thee quickly, and will fight against them with the sword of my mouth." (Revelation 2:16)

"And I will give [power] unto my two witnesses, and they shall prophesy a thousand two hundred [and] threescore days, clothed in sackcloth. These are the two olive trees, and the two candlesticks standing before the God of the earth. And if any man will hurt them, fire proceedeth out of their mouth, and devoureth their enemies: and if any man will hurt them, he must in this manner be killed. These have power to shut heaven, that it rain not in the days of their prophecy: and have power over waters to turn them to blood, and to smite the earth with all plagues, as often as they will." (Revelation 11:3-6)

"And out of his mouth goeth a sharp sword, that with it he should smite the nations: and he shall rule them with a rod of iron: and he treadeth the winepress of the fierceness and wrath of Almighty God." (Revelation 19:15)

By the Spirit of Christ and the Word spoken in faith, I deliver and set captives free, break chains that bind, remit the sins of those who have sinned against me, and undo heavy burdens. I don't hold grudges, rather I practice the same forgiveness that I have received from God. I also use this power to do what Jesus did by freeing those who are bound in any way. I help people to make peace with God, themselves, and with others.

"Whose soever sins ye remit, they are remitted unto them; [and] whose soever [sins] ye retain, they are retained." (John 20:23)

"Therefore if any man [be] in Christ, [he is] a new creature: old things are passed away; behold, all things are become new. And all things [are] of God, who hath reconciled us to himself by Jesus Christ, and hath given to us the ministry of reconciliation; To wit, that God was in Christ, reconciling the world unto himself, not imputing their trespasses unto them; and

hath committed unto us the word of reconciliation. Now then we are ambassadors for Christ, as though God did beseech [you] by us: we pray [you] in Christ's stead, be ye reconciled to God. For he hath made him [to be] sin for us, who knew no sin; that we might be made the righteousness of God in him." (2 Corinthians 5:17-21)

"And when ye stand praying, forgive, if ye have ought against any: that your Father also which is in heaven may forgive you your trespasses. But if ye do not forgive, neither will your Father which is in heaven forgive your trespasses." (Mark 11:25-26)

"Then his lord, after that he had called him, said unto him, O thou wicked servant, I forgave thee all that debt, because thou desiredst me: shouldest not thou also have had compassion on thy fellowservant, even as I had pity on thee? And his lord was wroth, and delivered him to the tormentors, till he should pay all that was due unto him. So likewise shall my heavenly Father do also unto you, if ye from your hearts forgive not every one his brother their trespasses." (Matthew 18:32-35)

"The Spirit of the Lord GOD [is] upon me; because the LORD hath anointed me to preach good tidings unto the meek; he hath sent me to bind up the brokenhearted, to proclaim liberty to the captives, and the opening of the prison to [them that are] bound; To proclaim the acceptable year of the LORD, and the day of vengeance of our God; to comfort all that mourn; To appoint unto them that mourn in Zion, to give unto them beauty for ashes, the oil of joy for mourning, the garment of praise for the spirit of heaviness; that they might be called trees of righteousness, the planting of the LORD, that he might be glorified." (Isaiah 61:1-3)

I pull down strongholds. The gates of hell and its counsels shall not prevail. I share in the ministry of Jesus Christ by ripping down the works of the devil and fighting a battle in the spirit realm that has immediate results in the physical world for those who were hemmed in and enslaved to the work of darkness in their lives.

> "(For the weapons of our warfare [are] not carnal, but mighty through God to the pulling down of strong holds;) *Casting down imaginations, and every high thing that exalteth itself against the knowledge of God, and bringing into captivity every thought to the obedience of Christ.*" (2 Corinthians 10:4-4)

> "*Now thanks [be] unto God, which always causeth us to triumph in Christ, and maketh manifest the savour of his knowledge by us in every place.*" (2 Corinthians 2:14)

> "*And Simon Peter answered and said, Thou art the Christ, the Son of the living God. And Jesus answered and said unto him, Blessed art thou, Simon Barjona: for flesh and blood hath not revealed [it] unto thee, but my Father which is in heaven. And I say also unto thee, That thou art Peter, and upon this rock I will build my church; and the gates of hell shall not prevail against it.*" (Matthew 16:16-18)

> "*He that committeth sin is of the devil; for the devil sinneth from the beginning. For this purpose the Son of God was manifested, that he might destroy the works of the devil.*" (1 John 3:8)

God's Words Can Be My Words

As God's ambassador and a citizen of the Kingdom of God, Elohim, God the creator's Word in my mouth is as powerful as His Word spoken by His mouth. I surrender my mouth and mind to God and speak out the words He gives me fearlessly, because it is His power that brings them to pass when I obey and work with Him. There are no limits when I function in the role and authority He has given me.

The creator's Word in my mouth is as powerful as His Word spoken by His mouth

"But the LORD said unto me, Say not, I [am] a child: for thou shalt go to all that I shall send thee, and whatsoever I command thee thou shalt speak...Then the LORD put forth his hand, and touched my mouth. And the LORD said unto me, Behold, I have put my words in thy mouth." (Jeremiah 1:7 and 9)

"But I [am] the LORD thy God, that divided the sea, whose waves roared: The LORD of hosts [is] his name. And I have put my words in thy mouth, and I have covered thee in the shadow of mine hand, that I may plant the heavens, and lay the foundations of the earth, and say unto Zion, Thou [art] my people." (Isaiah 51:15-16)

"As for me, this [is] my covenant with them, saith the LORD; My spirit that [is] upon thee, and my words which I have put in thy mouth, shall not depart out of thy mouth, nor out of the mouth of thy seed, nor out of the mouth of thy seed's seed, saith the LORD, from henceforth and for ever." (Isaiah 59:21)

"And the woman said to Elijah, Now by this I know that thou [art] a man of God, [and] that the word of the LORD in thy mouth [is] truth." (1Kings 17:24)

"Now therefore go, and I will be with thy mouth, and teach thee what thou shalt say." (Exodus 4:12)

"And the LORD said unto Moses, See, I have made thee a god to Pharaoh: and Aaron thy brother shall be thy prophet." (Exodus 7:1)

"And the LORD said unto Moses, Wherefore criest thou unto me? Speak unto the children of Israel, that they go forward:

but lift thou up thy rod, and stretch out thine hand over the sea, and divide it: and the children of Israel shall go on dry [ground] through the midst of the sea...And Israel saw that great work which the LORD did upon the Egyptians: and the people feared the LORD, and believed the LORD, and his servant Moses." (Exodus 14:15-16, and 31)

"Then spake Joshua to the LORD in the day when the LORD delivered up the Amorites before the children of Israel, and he said in the sight of Israel, Sun, stand thou still upon Gibeon; and thou, Moon, in the valley of Ajalon. And the sun stood still, and the moon stayed, until the people had avenged themselves upon their enemies. [Is] not this written in the book of Jasher? So the sun stood still in the midst of heaven, and hasted not to go down about a whole day. And there was no day like that before it or after it, that the LORD hearkened unto the voice of a man: for the LORD fought for Israel." (Joshua 10:12-14)

"Jesus answered them, Is it not written in your law, I said, Ye are gods?" (John 10:34)

"If any man speak, [let him speak] as the oracles of God; if any man minister, [let him do it] as of the ability which God giveth: that God in all things may be glorified through Jesus Christ, to whom be praise and dominion for ever and ever. Amen." (1 Peter 4:11)

"If ye abide in me, and my words abide in you, ye shall ask what ye will, and it shall be done unto you. Herein is my Father glorified, that ye bear much fruit; so shall ye be my disciples." (John 15:7-8)

"And I will give unto thee the keys of the kingdom of heaven: and whatsoever thou shalt bind on earth shall be bound in heaven: and whatsoever thou shalt loose on earth shall be loosed in heaven." (Matthew 16:19)

"Now unto him that is able to do exceeding abundantly above all that we ask or think, according to the power that worketh in us." (Ephesians 3:20)

"But we have this treasure in earthen vessels, that the excellency of the power may be of God, and not of us." (2 Corinthians 4:7)

"The Spirit itself beareth witness with our spirit, that we are the children of God: and if children, then heirs; heirs of God, and joint-heirs with Christ; if so be that we suffer with [him], that we may be also glorified together. For I reckon that the sufferings of this present time [are] not worthy [to be compared] with the glory which shall be revealed in us. For the earnest expectation of the creature waiteth for the manifestation of the sons of God." (Romans 8:16-19)

So shall my word be that goes forth out of my mouth; it shall accomplish that which I please and shall be successful in the matter to which I assign it. The words I utter out loud from my mouth under the anointing of the Spirit are not empty vessels or weak platitudes, but are powerful and unfailing to the glory of God.

"So shall my word be that goeth forth out of my mouth: it shall not return unto me void, but it shall accomplish that which I please, and it shall prosper [in the thing] whereto I sent it." (Isaiah 55:11)

"Thou shalt also decree a thing, and it shall be established unto thee: and the light shall shine upon thy ways." (Job 22:28)

Working in Concert with Angels

I request of God my Father and He dispatches ministering spirits. I don't have the authority to task God's loyal angels. There was one rebellion in heaven and there will not be another. The holy angels answer to God. However, as Jesus did in the time that He walked the earth as a man, I can make a request to God my Father in the name of Jesus for angelic assistance, and He will dispatch more than enough assistance to win the day. It is my God who sends His angels on assignment and I am a beneficiary of His grace and favor in this regard as were the Lord's servants of old and as are His children today.

"Thinkest thou that I cannot now pray to my Father, and he shall presently give me more than twelve legions of angels?" (Matthew 26:53)

"And in the sixth month the angel Gabriel was sent from God unto a city of Galilee, named Nazareth, to a virgin espoused to a man whose name was Joseph, of the house of David; and the virgin's name [was] Mary." (Luke 1:26-27)

"And when Peter was come to himself, he said, Now I know of a surety, that the Lord hath sent his angel, and hath delivered me out of the hand of Herod, and [from] all the expectation of the people of the Jews." (Acts 12:11)

"And he said unto me, These sayings [are] faithful and true: and the Lord God of the holy prophets sent his angel to shew unto his servants the things which must shortly be done." (Revelation 22:6)

"My God hath sent his angel, and hath shut the lions' mouths, that they have not hurt me: forasmuch as before him innocency was found in me; and also before thee, O king, have I done no hurt." (Daniel 6:22)

They are more and stronger that be with me than those that come against me and the Kingdom of God. I may not see them or even recognize their intervention until after a miracle, but there are more angels than a human mind can conceive that are ready to come to my aid when God gives them that assignment.

"And he answered, Fear not: for they that [be] with us [are] more than they that [be] with them." (2 Kings 6:16)

"But ye are come unto mount Sion, and unto the city of the living God, the heavenly Jerusalem, and to an innumerable company of angels." (Hebrews 12:22)

The holy angels of God minister to me. They harken to the voice of God's Word that I speak with faith, and God directs them to perform it. When I speak out the word and will of God with godlike faith, God my Father is pleased to give the angels marching orders to assist me, a son of God, and make things happen.

"Are they not all ministering spirits, sent forth to minister for them who shall be heirs of salvation?" (Hebrews 1:14)

"For he shall give his angels charge over thee, to keep thee in all thy ways." (Psalm 91:11)

"The angel of the LORD encampeth round about them that fear him, and delivereth them." (Psalm 34:7)

"Behold, I send an Angel before thee, to keep thee in the way, and to bring thee into the place which I have prepared." (Exodus 23:20)

"But the angel of the Lord by night opened the prison doors, and brought them forth, and said, Go, stand and speak in the temple to the people all the words of this life." (Acts 5:19-20)

"And when Herod would have brought him forth, the same night Peter was sleeping between two soldiers, bound with two chains: and the keepers before the door kept the prison. And, behold, the angel of the Lord came upon [him], and a light shined in the prison: and he smote Peter on the side, and raised him up, saying, Arise up quickly. And his chains fell off from [his] hands. And the angel said unto him, Gird thyself, and bind on thy sandals. And so he did. And he saith unto him, Cast thy garment about thee, and follow me. And he went out, and followed him; and wist not that it was true which was done by the angel; but thought he saw a vision. When

they were past the first and the second ward, they came unto the iron gate that leadeth unto the city; which opened to them of his own accord: and they went out, and passed on through one street; and forthwith the angel departed from him. And when Peter was come to himself, he said, Now I know of a surety, that the Lord hath sent his angel, and hath delivered me out of the hand of Herod, and [from] all the expectation of the people of the Jews." (Acts 12:6-11)

"Bless the LORD, ye his angels, that excel in strength, that do his commandments, hearkening unto the voice of his word." (Psalm 103:20)

Say It Out Loud, On Purpose, and In Faith

I believe that I receive. I take my requests to God as a done deal. I believe that I have already received my petitions when I make them and God honors His promises to me.

"And Samuel grew, and the LORD was with him, and did let none of his words fall to the ground." (1 Samuel 3:19)

"And whatsoever we ask, we receive of him, because we keep his commandments, and do those things that are pleasing in his sight." (1 John 3:22)

"But without faith [it is] impossible to please [him]: for he that cometh to God must believe that he is, and [that] he is a rewarder of them that diligently seek him." (Hebrews 11:6)

"Jesus saith unto her, Said I not unto thee, that, if thou wouldest believe, thou shouldest see the glory of God?" (John 11:40)

"Therefore I say unto you, What things soever ye desire, when ye pray, believe that ye receive [them], and ye shall have [them]." (Mark 11:24)

Life is in the power of my tongue. I love it and eat the fruit of it. I am made in the image of God. He has called me His son. The unique Son of God, Jesus Christ, shares His power with me. God cannot lie because reality conforms to His words. Likewise, I have been given the creative power to speak things into existence, in alignment with the will of God, for His glory. The same process that operated when I spoke out my belief in God for the purpose of salvation works to bring deliverance on other occasions when, in faith, I speak out loud the will of God and honor the God who gets things done.

I have been given the creative power to speak things into existence

"The tongue of the just [is as] choice silver: the heart of the wicked [is] little worth. The lips of the righteous feed many: but fools die for want of wisdom." (Proverbs 10:20-21)

"Death and life [are] in the power of the tongue: and they that love it shall eat the fruit thereof." (Proverbs 18:21)

"A good man out of the good treasure of the heart bringeth forth good things: and an evil man out of the evil treasure bringeth forth evil things." (Matthew 12:35)

"But what saith it? The word is nigh thee, [even] in thy mouth, and in thy heart: that is, the word of faith, which we preach; that if thou shalt confess with thy mouth the Lord Jesus, and shalt believe in thine heart that God hath raised him from the dead, thou shalt be saved. For with the heart man believeth unto righteousness; and with the mouth confession is made unto salvation." (Romans 10:8-10)

I have what I say. I see it with the eye of faith and the images I conceive and meditate upon in my thoughts are established and manifested in this realm as in heaven. I see with the eye of the spirit what God shows me, keep it before me in my thoughts as real and complete, then fearlessly speak out decreeing what I see as though it were already done. I then maintain that image and faith until I see it done in the physical realm.

The images I conceive and meditate upon in my thoughts are established and manifested

"For which cause we faint not; but though our outward man perish, yet the inward [man] is renewed day by day. For our light affliction, which is but for a moment, worketh for us a far more exceeding [and] eternal weight of glory; while we look not at the things which are seen, but at the things which are not seen: for the things which are seen [are] temporal; but the things which are not seen [are] eternal." (2 Corinthians 4:16-18)

"And Jesus answering saith unto them, Have faith in God. For verily I say unto you, That whosoever shall say unto this mountain, Be thou removed, and be thou cast into the sea; and shall not doubt in his heart, but shall believe that those things which he saith shall come to pass; he shall have whatsoever he saith. Therefore I say unto you, What things soever ye desire, when ye pray, believe that ye receive [them], and ye shall have [them]." (Mark 11:22-24)

"If ye abide in me, and my words abide in you, ye shall ask what ye will, and it shall be done unto you." (John 15:7)

"Thou shalt also decree a thing, and it shall be established unto thee: and the light shall shine upon thy ways." (Job 22:28)

"Now faith is the substance of things hoped for, the evidence of things not seen...Through faith we understand that the worlds were framed by the word of God, so that things which are seen were not made of things which do appear." (Hebrews 11:1)

"Then answered Jesus and said unto them, Verily, verily, I say unto you, The Son can do nothing of himself, but what he seeth the Father do: for what things soever he doeth, these also doeth the Son likewise. For the Father loveth the Son, and sheweth him all things that himself doeth: and he will shew him greater works than these, that ye may marvel." (John 5:19-20)

"I speak that which I have seen with my Father: and ye do that which ye have seen with your father." (John 8:38)

"Now unto him that is able to do exceeding abundantly above all that we ask or think, according to the power that worketh in us." (Ephesians 3:20)

"(Beforetime in Israel, when a man went to enquire of God, thus he spake, Come, and let us go to the seer: for [he that is] now [called] a Prophet was beforetime called a Seer.)" (1 Samuel 9:9)

"A good man out of the good treasure of his heart bringeth forth that which is good; and an evil man out of the evil treasure of his heart bringeth forth that which is evil: for of the abundance of the heart his mouth speaketh." (Luke 6:45)

"And it shall come to pass afterward, [that] I will pour out my spirit upon all flesh; and your sons and your daughters shall prophesy, your old men shall dream dreams, your young men shall see visions." (Joel 2:28)

"Be careful for nothing; but in every thing by prayer and supplication with thanksgiving let your requests be made known unto God. And the peace of God, which passeth all understanding, shall keep your hearts and minds through Christ Jesus. Finally, brethren, whatsoever things are true, whatsoever things [are] honest, whatsoever things [are] just, whatsoever things [are] pure, whatsoever things [are] lovely, whatsoever things [are] of good report; if [there be] any virtue,

and if [there be] any praise, think on these things." (Philippians 4:6-8)

I agree with the Word of God. I obtain the promises of God. I maintain alignment with God's word in the Holy Bible. The promises He energizes within me are in perfect alignment with the written word. I don't move from that place of alignment, but rather affirm it by speaking it out loud in faith and strengthen my faith in His promises. I then receive what God has promised.

"But whoso keepeth his word, in him verily is the love of God perfected: hereby know we that we are in him." (1 John 2:5)

"Cast not away therefore your confidence, which hath great recompence of reward." (Hebrews 10:35)

"Grace and peace be multiplied unto you through the knowledge of God, and of Jesus our Lord, According as his divine power hath given unto us all things that [pertain] unto life and godliness, through the knowledge of him that hath called us to glory and virtue: whereby are given unto us exceeding great and precious promises: that by these ye might be partakers of the divine nature, having escaped the corruption that is in the world through lust. And beside this, giving all diligence, add to your faith virtue; and to virtue knowledge; and to knowledge temperance; and to temperance patience; and to patience godliness; and to godliness brotherly kindness; and to brotherly kindness charity. For if these things be in you, and abound, they make [you that ye shall] neither [be] barren nor unfruitful in the knowledge of our Lord Jesus Christ." (2 Peter 1:2-8)

"Let us hold fast the profession of [our] faith without wavering; (for he [is] faithful that promised)." (Hebrews 10:23

"Jesus saith unto her, Said I not unto thee, that, if thou wouldest believe, thou shouldest see the glory of God?" (John 11:40)

CHAPTER 12
I CALL SPECIFIC PERSONAL
DESIRES INTO EXISTENCE

Write Out and Decree Your Future

I take hold of my inheritance. My personal desires are my own. I have chosen not to put them into print as some might misunderstand. I will say that some desires have already been fulfilled. I encourage the reader to specifically write down personal desires after prayerfully receiving the peace of God that none of those things would pull you away from God. Likewise, it would be even better if those things can be submitted to and used by God for kingdom purposes.

Kingdom purposes

"But seek ye first the kingdom of God, and his righteousness; and all these things shall be added unto you." (Matthew 6:33)

"In whom also we have obtained an inheritance, being predestinated according to the purpose of him who worketh all things after the counsel of his own will: that we should be to the praise of his glory, who first trusted in Christ." (Ephesians 1:11-12)

"Ye lust, and have not: ye kill, and desire to have, and cannot obtain: ye fight and war, yet ye have not, because ye ask not." (James 4:2)

"My people are destroyed for lack of knowledge: because thou hast rejected knowledge, I will also reject thee, that thou shalt be no priest to me: seeing thou hast forgotten the law of thy God, I will also forget thy children." (Hosea 4:6)

"But thou, when thou prayest, enter into thy closet, and when thou hast shut thy door, pray to thy Father which is in secret; and thy Father which seeth in secret shall reward thee openly." (Matthew 6:6)

"And it shall be, when the LORD thy God shall have brought thee into the land which he sware unto thy fathers, to Abraham, to Isaac, and to Jacob, to give thee great and goodly cities, which thou buildedst not, and houses full of all good [things], which thou filledst not, and wells digged, which thou diggedst not, vineyards and olive trees, which thou plantedst not; when thou shalt have eaten and be full." (Deuteronomy 6:10-11)

"Beware that thou forget not the LORD thy God, in not keeping his commandments, and his judgments, and his statutes, which I command thee this day: lest [when] thou hast eaten and art full, and hast built goodly houses, and dwelt [therein]; and [when] thy herds and thy flocks multiply, and thy silver and thy gold is multiplied, and all that thou hast is multiplied; then thine heart be lifted up, and thou forget the LORD thy God, which brought thee forth out of the land of Egypt, from the house of bondage." (Deuteronomy 8:11-14)

"And the LORD shall make thee plenteous in goods, in the fruit of thy body, and in the fruit of thy cattle, and in the fruit of thy ground, in the land which the LORD sware unto thy fathers to give thee." (Deuteronomy 28:11)

CHAPTER 13
MY TIME, MY PERSONAL CALLING, MISSION, AND ASSIGNMENTS

My set time and the seasons of my visitation have arrived. God has given me money with a mission; prosperity with a purpose. I have the resources and use them to build and run orphanages to care for orphaned children, raise them to know and receive Christ, and to raise up Christian workers from them; to build and run housing for seniors, the poor, widows, and the disabled, that include chapels, offer Bible studies, and provide for organized intercessory prayer. And I have all kinds of profits from real estate investments in general. I develop and patent a breakthrough device and receive great wealth from fees and royalties. I fund and dispatch ministry and healing teams. I am a forerunner for international evangelistic campaigns. I heal and minister deliverance by the Spirit of Yahweh Rophe, God my healer. I sing, compose, play Christian music, and write Christian books like The Epic of God and According to Your Word Lord, I Pray. I support witnesses, and their families, who do not fear persecution and who are prepared to become martyrs for the sake of the gospel by refusing to be spared by denying Christ. I give generously to every good work yet I am not diminished.

There is a Set Time

My set time and the seasons of my visitation have arrived. This is the time that God has set to move in my life, by the Spirit, in extraordinary ways.

"But ye [are] a chosen generation, a royal priesthood, an holy nation, a peculiar people; that ye should shew forth the praises of him who hath called you out of darkness into his marvelous light: which in time past [were] not a people, but [are] now the people of God: which had not obtained mercy, but now have obtained mercy. Dearly beloved, I beseech [you] as strangers and pilgrims, abstain from fleshly lusts, which war against the soul; Having your conversation honest among the Gentiles: that, whereas they speak against you as evildoers, they may by [your] good works, which they shall behold, glorify God in the day of visitation." (1 Peter 2:9-12)

"Arise, shine; for thy light is come, and the glory of the LORD is risen upon thee." (Isaiah 60:1)

"Thou shalt arise, [and] have mercy upon Zion: for the time to favour her, yea, the set time, is come." (Psalm 102:13)

Calling, Mission, and Assignments

God has made me to be a king in the marketplace and has given me money with a mission; prosperity with a purpose. I am a multi-millionaire many times over. God has already given me my first million dollars in savings, stocks, and bonds. That is apart from counting my overall positive net worth when including physical assets used in daily living for shelter and transportation. It is only the beginning because God can trust me with increased wealth to use it for the Kingdom of God. That is a major change for the poor little boy whose family was on welfare, whose food was basic and limited, as was clothing and heat for the brutal Chicago winters of my youth.

"And the LORD shall make thee the head, and not the tail; and thou shalt be above only, and thou shalt not be beneath; if that thou hearken unto the commandments of the LORD thy God, which I command thee this day, to observe and to do [them]." (Deuteronomy 28:13)

"Fear not, little flock; for it is your Father's good pleasure to give you the kingdom." (Luke 12:32)

"Ye are the light of the world. A city that is set on an hill cannot be hid. Neither do men light a candle, and put it under a bushel, but on a candlestick; and it giveth light unto all that are in the house. Let your light so shine before men, that they may see your good works, and glorify your Father which is in heaven." (Matthew 5:14-16)

"Thou shalt increase my greatness, and comfort me on every side." (Psalm 71:21)

"Not slothful in business; fervent in spirit; serving the Lord; Rejoicing in hope; patient in tribulation; continuing instant in prayer; Distributing to the necessity of saints; given to hospitality." (Romans 12:11-13)

"In the house of the righteous [is] much treasure: but in the revenues of the wicked is trouble." (Proverbs 15:6)

I have the resources and use them to build and run orphanages to care for orphaned children, raise them to know and receive Christ, and to raise up Christian workers from them; to build and run housing for seniors, the poor, widows, and the disabled, that include chapels, offer Bible studies, and provide for organized intercessory prayer. I have a vision and plan for what to do with increased resources. By faith, I call those resources in so that I can put them to work in the Kingdom of God. Once, when I was on a church outing in the southern portion of Western Australia, I stumbled upon an abandoned brick building in the woods, seemingly in the middle of nowhere. My Australian pastor explained to me that it was one of the orphanages that the great George Mueller had set up. I didn't know who George Mueller was at the time. However, in recent years, as the desire to care for orphans began to take hold of me, I began to study the life and faith of Mueller. God cares for the orphan and uses his people to directly care for them. It is something that burns within me to do also.

"Pure religion and undefiled before God and the Father is this, to visit the fatherless and widows in their affliction, [and] to keep himself unspotted from the world." (James 1:27)

"Learn to do well; seek judgment, relieve the oppressed, judge the fatherless, plead for the widow. Come now, and let us reason together, saith the LORD: though your sins be as scarlet, they shall be as white as snow; though they be red like crimson, they shall be as wool. If ye be willing and obedient, ye shall eat the good of the land." (Isaiah 1:17-19)

"Thus speaketh the LORD of hosts, saying, Execute true judgment, and shew mercy and compassions every man to his brother: and oppress not the widow, nor the fatherless, the stranger, nor the poor; and let none of you imagine evil against his brother in your heart." (Zechariah 7:9-10)

"And whoso shall receive one such little child in my name receiveth me." (Matthew 18:5)

"A father of the fatherless, and a judge of the widows, [is] God in his holy habitation. God setteth the solitary in families: he bringeth out those which are bound with chains: but the rebellious dwell in a dry [land]." (Psalm 68:5-6)

"Defend the poor and fatherless: do justice to the afflicted and needy. Deliver the poor and needy: rid [them] out of the hand of the wicked." (Psalm 82:3-3)

And I have all kinds of profits from real estate investments in general. There are many ways to increase wealth from investments in real estate. Real property is part of the blessing of God that I receive by faith and obedience to His leading.

"And Jesus answered and said, Verily I say unto you, There is no man that hath left house, or brethren, or sisters, or father, or mother, or wife, or children, or lands, for my sake, and the gospel's, but he shall receive an hundredfold now in this time,

houses, and brethren, and sisters, and mothers, and children, and lands, with persecutions; and in the world to come eternal life." (Mark 10:29-30)

I develop and patent a breakthrough device and receive great wealth from fees and royalties. Through history men like Alexander Graham Bell, the inventor of the telephone, and Henry Ford, who developed a process to mass produce automobiles, have developed innovations that changed the way people live and do business. These innovations brought them great wealth. I receive from God the secrets to an innovative device that is a game changer in our time. I use the wealth from that for the Kingdom of God.

> *"I wisdom dwell with prudence, and find out knowledge of witty inventions."* (Proverbs 8:12)

I fund and dispatch ministry and healing teams. My capacity to fund the works of God is increased and deployed in His service.

> *"Honour the LORD with thy substance, and with the first-fruits of all thine increase: So shall thy barns be filled with plenty, and thy presses shall burst out with new wine."* (Proverbs 3:9-10)

> *"And I will make of thee a great nation, and I will bless thee, and make thy name great; and thou shalt be a blessing: and I will bless them that bless thee, and curse him that curseth thee: and in thee shall all families of the earth be blessed."* (Genesis 12:2-2)

I am a forerunner for international evangelistic campaigns. I have had a small taste of being part of an international evangelistic campaign and have also supported such campaigns with prayers and finances. However, I see myself in a new and larger role.

"After these things the Lord appointed other seventy also, and sent them two and two before his face into every city and place, whither he himself would come." (Luke 10:1)

I heal and minister deliverance by the Spirit of Yahweh Rophe, God my healer. When Jesus walked the earth as a man there was great activity by demonic spirits. Jesus took authority over that surge of demonic power freeing people from its torment. He has given us the same authority and calling. It is clear that evil angels are active in our world and are behind the outrageous events, bondage, and bloodshed that has been chronicled in history books and in contemporary news media. There have been instances in the past that God has used me in this ministry of deliverance, but a greater role is before me.

"And heal the sick that are therein, and say unto them, The kingdom of God is come nigh unto you...And the seventy returned again with joy, saying, Lord, even the devils are subject unto us through thy name. And he said unto them, I beheld Satan as lightning fall from heaven. Behold, I give unto you power to tread on serpents and scorpions, and over all the power of the enemy: and nothing shall by any means hurt you." (Luke 10:9 and 17-19)

"[[A Psalm] of David.] Bless the LORD, O my soul: and all that is within me, [bless] his holy name. Bless the LORD, O my soul, and forget not all his benefits: who forgiveth all thine iniquities; who healeth all thy diseases." (Psalm 103:1-3)

"Surely he hath borne our griefs, and carried our sorrows: yet we did esteem him stricken, smitten of God, and afflicted. But he [was] wounded for our transgressions, [he was] bruised for our iniquities: the chastisement of our peace [was] upon him; and with his stripes we are healed." (Isaiah 53:4-5)

"And [his] brightness was as the light; he had horns [coming] out of his hand: and there [was] the hiding of his power." (Habakkuk 3:4)

I sing, compose, play Christian music, and write Christian books like The Epic of God and According to Your Word Lord, I Pray. Rather than seek further advancement in my previous secular career, I repeatedly told God my Father that I wanted to work for Him. It is happening and I am thrilled by it.

"*Sing unto him a new song; play skilfully with a loud noise.*"
(Psalm 33:3)

I support witnesses, and their families, who do not fear persecution and who are prepared to become martyrs for the sake of the gospel by refusing to be spared by denying Christ. The persecution of Christian believers wasn't limited to the first two centuries after Jesus gave His life to remove the sins of those who would believe on Him and open the way for eternal fellowship with the Godhead. Inquisitions, wars, and evil representatives of the kingdom of darkness have taken a toll on those who considered their lives a light matter rather than to deny the faith of Jesus Christ. It is not over. So I am compelled to support these brave witnesses and their families with prayer, action, and finances.

"*Who [is] he that condemneth? [It is] Christ that died, yea rather, that is risen again, who is even at the right hand of God, who also maketh intercession for us. Who shall separate us from the love of Christ? [shall] tribulation, or distress, or persecution, or famine, or nakedness, or peril, or sword? As it is written, For thy sake we are killed all the day long; we are accounted as sheep for the slaughter. Nay, in all these things we are more than conquerors through him that loved us. For I am persuaded, that neither death, nor life, nor angels, nor principalities, nor powers, nor things present, nor things to come, nor height, nor depth, nor any other creature, shall be able to separate us from the love of God, which is in Christ Jesus our Lord.*" (Romans 8:34-39)

"For I think that God hath set forth us the apostles last, as it were appointed to death: for we are made a spectacle unto the world, and to angels, and to men." (1 Corinthians 4:9)

I give generously to every good work yet I am not diminished. I take joy in looking back at the amounts of my resources I have given to the Kingdom of God. I am overjoyed by the thought of the significant gifts I have yet to give, but will be empowered to give, without coming to the end of my resources. God's promise of overflowing blessings is not for waste or for ostentatious self-absorbed displays, but for blessing others from that flow and financing the agenda of the kingdom and His workers.

God's promise of overflowing blessings is not for waste...but for blessing others

"And God [is] able to make all grace abound toward you; that ye, always having all sufficiency in all [things], may abound to every good work: (As it is written, He hath dispersed abroad; he hath given to the poor: his righteousness remaineth for ever. Now he that ministereth seed to the sower both minister bread for [your] food, and multiply your seed sown, and increase the fruits of your righteousness;) *Being enriched in every thing to all bountifulness, which causeth through us thanksgiving to God."* (2 Corinthians 9:8-11)

"There is that scattereth, and yet increaseth; and [there is] that withholdeth more than is meet, but [it tendeth] to poverty." (Proverbs 11:24)

CHAPTER 14
I ASK AND THEN THANK GOD FOR WHAT HAS BEEN CONFESSED AS ALREADY DONE

I decree these things and they are established! I ask You, God my Father, to grant my petitions and to bring my words to pass. I ask this of You in Jesus' name, the Apostle and High Priest of my confession. I thank you God my Father, Abba, Daddy, that it is done, settled, established, and a present reality on earth as it is in heaven. Amen.

Consider It Done!

I decree these things and they are established! I decree the things detailed in this prayerful decree and call them done!

> *"So shall my word be that goeth forth out of my mouth: it shall not return unto me void, but it shall accomplish that which I please, and it shall prosper [in the thing] whereto I sent it."* (Isaiah 5:11)

> *"And Jesus answering saith unto them, Have faith in God. For verily I say unto you, That whosoever shall say unto this mountain, Be thou removed, and be thou cast into the sea; and shall not doubt in his heart, but shall believe that those things which he saith shall come to pass; he shall have whatsoever he*

165

saith. Therefore I say unto you, what things soever ye desire, when ye pray, believe that ye receive [them], and ye shall have [them]." (Mark 11:22-24)

"Acquaint now thyself with him, and be at peace: thereby good shall come unto thee. Receive, I pray thee, the law from his mouth, and lay up his words in thine heart. If thou return to the Almighty, thou shalt be built up, thou shalt put away iniquity far from thy tabernacles. Then shalt thou lay up gold as dust, and the [gold] of Ophir as the stones of the brooks. Yea, the Almighty shall be thy defence, and thou shalt have plenty of silver. For then shalt thou have thy delight in the Almighty, and shalt lift up thy face unto God. Thou shalt make thy prayer unto him, and he shall hear thee, and thou shalt pay thy vows. Thou shalt also decree a thing, and it shall be established unto thee: and the light shall shine upon thy ways." (Job 22:21-28)

I ask You, God my Father, to grant my petitions and to bring my words to pass. I take Jesus at His word and boldly ask God my Father to grant the requests I have petitioned of Him in the name of Jesus.

Boldly ask God

"Thus saith the LORD, the Holy One of Israel, and his Maker, Ask me of things to come concerning my sons, and concerning the work of my hands command ye me." (Isaiah 45:11)

"And this is the confidence that we have in him, that, if we ask any thing according to his will, he heareth us: and if we know that he hear us, whatsoever we ask, we know that we have the petitions that we desired of him." (1 John 5:14-15)

"And Jabez called on the God of Israel, saying, Oh that thou wouldest bless me indeed, and enlarge my coast, and that thine hand might be with me, and that thou wouldest keep

[me] from evil, that it may not grieve me! And God granted him that which he requested." (1 Chronicles 4:10)

"Hitherto have ye asked nothing in my name: ask, and ye shall receive, that your joy may be full." (John 16:24)

I ask this of You in Jesus' name, the Apostle and High Priest of my confession. I make my petition in the name of Jesus, taking Him at His word as to the certainty of what I have requested and decreed, when I do so in faith, of all that He is and what He taught me to do.

"Wherefore, holy brethren, partakers of the heavenly calling, consider the Apostle and High Priest of our profession, Christ Jesus." (Hebrews 3:1)

"Having therefore, brethren, boldness to enter into the holiest by the blood of Jesus, by a new and living way, which he hath consecrated for us, through the veil, that is to say, his flesh; and [having] an high priest over the house of God; let us draw near with a true heart in full assurance of faith, having our hearts sprinkled from an evil conscience, and our bodies washed with pure water. Let us hold fast the profession of [our] faith without wavering; (for he [is] faithful that promised)." (Hebrews 10:19-23)

"Believest thou not that I am in the Father, and the Father in me? The words that I speak unto you I speak not of myself: but the Father that dwelleth in me, he doeth the works. Believe me that I [am] in the Father, and the Father in me: or else believe me for the very works' sake. Verily, verily, I say unto you, He that believeth on me, the works that I do shall he do also; and greater [works] than these shall he do; because I go unto my Father. And whatsoever ye shall ask in my name, that will I do, that the Father may be glorified in the Son. If ye shall ask any thing in my name, I will do [it]." (John 14:10-14)

I thank you God my Father, Abba, Daddy, that it is done, settled, established, and a present reality on earth as it is in heaven. Amen. I rejoice in thanksgiving and praise that God my Father, my dear Daddy in heaven, will do even as I have asked in the confidence that He does not lie, that He loves His children, and that He is pleased that I have the confidence to approach Him, believe Him, and without my own misguided self-imposed limits, ask in faith for my heart's desire.

"God [is] not a man, that he should lie; neither the son of man, that he should repent: hath he said, and shall he not do [it]? or hath he spoken, and shall he not make it good?" (Numbers 23:19)

"After this manner therefore pray ye: Our Father which art in heaven, Hallowed be thy name. Thy kingdom come. Thy will be done in earth, as [it is] in heaven." (Matthew 6:9-10)

"And from the days of John the Baptist until now the kingdom of heaven suffereth violence, and the violent take it by force." (Matthew 11:12)

"Ask, and it shall be given you; seek, and ye shall find; knock, and it shall be opened unto you: For every one that asketh receiveth; and he that seeketh findeth; and to him that knocketh it shall be opened...If ye then, being evil, know how to give good gifts unto your children, how much more shall your Father which is in heaven give good things to them that ask him?" (Matthew 7:7-8 and 11)

CHAPTER 15
MAKE PEACE WITH GOD

Time for the Most Important Thing

This book was written for believers. However, if you have not yet made peace with God, you can take care of that unfinished business right now. You can't expect to operate the promises of God absent a personal relationship with the God who made those promises. If you lack, but want that relationship with God then please pray the following prayer.

Dear God, I have made a mess of my life without You. I am sorry for all of the wrong things I have done, said, or thought. I am also sorry for the things I could have done to help others yet failed to do because I closed my heart and my hand. Please forgive me. I believe in You and purpose to honor the Godhead of the Father, Son, and Holy Spirit with my life, obedience, and resources. Cleanse me with the blood of Jesus and come live in me. Give me the power to become Your child and to faithfully do Your will. Thank you for hearing my prayer. I thank You that, according to Your word, I am now saved from the path of destruction and from a wayward, aimless life to a life of forgiveness from sin, right standing with God, and the joy of eternal life with You that begins now! In the name of Jesus I pray, amen.

Cleanse me with the blood of Jesus and come live in me

If you have said that prayer and believed it in your heart. I encourage you to build on your new relationship with God through daily prayer, habitually reading the Bible, seeking to know God and His ways better, and finding a good church to attend regularly. Tell others about your decision and ask to be baptized.

Welcome to the family of God!

ENDNOTES

1. Luke 11:2; John 4:23

2. Genesis 21:33; Isaiah 40:28

3. Exodus 3:13-15

4. Jeremiah 29:12; 33:3

5. Numbers 23:19; Deuteronomy 7:9; 15:5-6; Joshua 23:14; 2 Samuel 7:28; 1 Kings 8:56; 1 Chronicles 17:26-27; 2 Chronicles 7:14; Psalm 89:34; 81:10; 118:4-6; 119:49 (Amplified); 119:58, 114, and 165; 121:7-8; Isaiah 43:26; Jeremiah 33:3; Joel 2:25; Matthew 11:28; 12:21;18:19; John 3:16; 11:25-26 and 40; 14:12-14; 15:7; 16:23-24; Acts 2:39; 27:25; Romans 4:20-21; 15:4; 2 Corinthians 1:20; 6:16 through 7:1; Galatians 3:13-14 and 29; Ephesians 1:13-14; Titus 1:2; Hebrews 6:12-19; 10:23; 2 Peter 1:4; 1 John 2:25; 3:21-22; 5:14-15; James 1:12; 4:8;

6. Genesis 17:1-2 and 7; Romans 4:16; Galatians 3:7-9 and 29

7. 2 Chronicles 20:7; John 15:13-15; James 2:23

8. Romans 8:14-17 and 32; Galatians 4:7

9. Genesis 14:19; Psalm 9:2; Daniel 7:18, 22, and 25; Luke 6:35; John 1:12-13; Romans 8:14-17; Ephesians 5:1; 1 John 5:1-2; Revelation 21:7

10. Genesis 1:26-27; 3:5; 32:28; Exodus 7:1; Joshua 10: 12-13;

Matthew 8:27; 19:28; Mark 11:22-24 (Wycliffe Bible, Young's Literal Translation, and the Message Bible); John 6:28-29; 10:34-36; 14:12; 14:21-23; 17:20-24; Ephesians 2:4-6; 4:13 and 24 (Good News Translation); 3:16-19; Romans 8:14-17; 8:29; Hebrews 1:14; II Peter 1:3-4; Revelation 21:6-7

11. 2 Corinthians 5:17-21; Revelation 17:1-2

12. Proverbs 29:2; Luke 11:2

13. I Peter 2:9; Revelation 1:5-6

14. Isaiah 61:1-3 and 6-7; 2 Corinthians 6:4

15. Matthew 6:9-10

16. Isaiah 37:21-22; 62:6-7 (Amplified); Ezekiel 3:17; 33:7; 1 Corinthians 3:9 and 4:1; 2 Corinthians 6:1

17. Psalm 149:6-9; Isaiah 6:8; Ezekiel 22:30; Ephesians 6:6 and 18; John 4:23

18. Job 22:28; Psalm 60:12; Jeremiah 20:9; 42:4; Ezekiel 3:4; Amos 7:15

19. Isaiah 6:8; Micah 4:1-2; Habakkuk 3:4 (Amplified); Matthew 28:19; Mark 1:38; Luke 19:10; John 6:28; 9:3-4; 13:34; 14:10-14; Acts 19:11; 2 Corinthians 10:4 (NAS)

20. Ephesians 6:18

21. James 5:16

22. Genesis 1:31; 2:2; 12:2-3; 14:19 and 30; 14:22; 17:1; 18:1-2; 18:14; 45:7; Exodus 3:14; 15:3; 15: 7 and 11; 15:11 and 26; 19:5 and 6; 20:3-5; 34:5-7;34:6 and 10; 34:14; Leviticus 20:26; 21:8; Numbers 8:17; 14:18; Deuteronomy 4:15; 7:9; 4:24; 29:29; 33:27-29; Joshua 10:10-11and 14; Ruth 3:9; 2 Samuel 22:2-4; 1 Kings 8:23; 1 Chronicles 16:27; 29:11; 29:17; 2 Chronicles 2:6; 20:29; Nehemiah 1:5 (NIV); 8:10; Job 5:17-18; 34:17 (NIV); 36:5; 37:22-23; 40:2; 42:2; Psalm 1:1-3; 3:3; 3:6; 4:3-5; 8:1 and 3; 9:2; 9:9-10; 16:11; 18:28; 18:30; 19:9-11; 21:13; 23:2 and 3; 23; 27:4; 27:5; 27:4; 33:8 and 11; 36:5-7 and 9; 37:3; 50:1; 50:21-23; 63:3; 68:19; 72:18 (NIV); 75:6-7; 77:14 (NIV); 78:10-12; 83:18; 84:11; 86:5, 10 and

15; 91:1, 2, 3, 15, and 16; 94:1; 99:8; 103:2-3; 107:2; 138:8; 139:1-4
and 23; 139:7-10; 139:23-24; 140:7; 142:7; 143:10; 145:6-9 and 17;
147:3 and 5; Proverbs 3:11-12; 8:30-31; 10:22; Song of Solomon
1:2-4; Isaiah 7:14; 9:6 and 7; 11:2; 30:18; 33:14; 35:2; 42:2; 42:8
and 16; 45:21; 45:21-23; 46:13 (NIV); 47:4; 48:10; 48:17; 49:7;
49:17 (NIV); 53:2; 54:8; 55:8-9; 57:15; 59:16; 60:16; 61:1; 63:9;
63:12 (NIV); 66:11-13; Jeremiah 1:5; 2:8, 9, 13 and 35; 9:24
(Amplified); 11:20; 17:13; 23:5; 29:11 (NIV); 29:11; 29:13; 32:21;
32:27; Ezekiel 3:16-21; 14:20; Daniel 7:18 and 22; 9:4 (NIV);
Joel 2:13; 2:25-26; Amos 3:7; Nahum 1:2-7; Zephaniah 3:17;
Malachi 3:3; 3:6; 4:2; Matthew 1:23; 5:48; 8:2-3; 8:27; 11:28-
29; 12:25; 12:50; 14:14; 15:32; 16:24; 17:1-2; 18:4; 18:32-35; 19:16;
19:26; 21:5; 28:20; Mark 1:41; 2:19-20; 4:11; 5:20; Luke 2:10-11;
5:34-35; 6:35; 8:46; 18:1-8; 22:24-30; 22:44; John 1:1-4 and 7;
1:29; 3:16 and 17; 3:8; 3:16; 4:10 and 14 and 24; 5:20; 6:28; 6:35;
6:37; 6:53-56; 7:37-41; 8:15-17; 10:11; 6:33-35 and 48-58; 10:7-9
and 11; 10:27-30; 13:13; 13:19; 14:6; 14:10-12; 14:13-14; 14:16-17;
15:1-2; 15:13-15; 16:13-15 and 23-24; 16:27; 17:15; 17:17; Acts 10:10-
16; 22:17-18; Romans 1:20; 8:14-17; 8:27; 8:29; 8:39; 9:15; 12:19;
14:11;Philippians 2:5-11; 3:10; Ephesians 1:17 and 18; 3:17-19;
Colossians 3:12-15; 1 Corinthians 2:7 and 10; 10:22; 12:3; 13:4-
7; 15:54-57; 2 Corinthians 1:3-4; 3:18; 5:17; 5:19 and 20; 13:11;
Galatians 2:20; 3:13-14; 5:1 and 22-23; Ephesians 3:3-6; 4:30;
Philippians 1:6; Colossians 1:15; 1Thessalonians 5:23 and 24; 2
Thessalonians 3:5; 1 Timothy 1:1 and 17; 2:5-6; 4:10; 2 Timothy
1:9-10; 2:13; Hebrews 2:9; 3:1; 4:12; 4:13; 4:14-16; 6:17-18; 9:11-15;
9:14-15; 10:9; 10:11-12 and 21; 11:6; 11:27; 13:20 and 21; 12:2; 12:24;
12:29; 13:20-21; James 1:17; 3:17; 4:8; 5:10; 1 Peter 1: 3,4 and 15;
1:23 (NIV); 5:7-10; 2 Peter 1:3-4 and 16-17; 1:11; 3:9; 1 John 1:5;
2:1 and 20; 3:3 and 7; 4:8-10, and 16; 5:20; 4:12; Jude v. 24-25;
Revelation 1:4; 2:23; 4:11; 5: 9-10 and 13;7:9-17; 10:7; 15:3; 19:6-7;
19:11-16; 21:2-7; 22:17

23. Deuteronomy 23:5; Mark 10:21; John 3:16; 14:21 and 23; 15:9;
16:26-27; 17:23 and 26; 2 Corinthians 13:14; 2 Thessalonians
2:16; 1 John 4:7-10 and 16; Revelation 1:5

24. John 10:11; Galatians 3:13-14; Ephesians 3:18-19; Hebrews 13:20-21

25. John 14:15-17 and 26

26. Ephesians 4:30; I Thessalonians 5:19

27. Proverbs 18:24; Isaiah 61:1-3, 6-7, and 10; 2 Corinthians 13:14 (Message); Ephesians 3:19 (Amplified); 1 John 3:8

28. Deuteronomy 5:25; 1 Chronicles 16:11; Psalm 9:10 (Amplified); 27:8; 42:1; 57:5-11; 108:1; Isaiah 26:9; Jeremiah 9:24; 29:13; Matthew 5:8; 6:33; 7:7-8; Colossians 3:1; Hebrews 12:2

29. Genesis 12:7; 17:1-3; 18:1; 26:2 and 24; 35:1, 9, 14 and 15; 46:2 and 3; Exodus 3:2-6; Leviticus 9:3 and 4, 23 and 24; Numbers 12:5-8; Deuteronomy 31:15; Judges 6:11-14, 22 and 23; 13:16-23; 1 Kings 3:5-14; 9:1 and 2; 22:19; 2 Chronicles 1:7; 7:12-14; Job 19:25-27; Psalm 27:4 and 8; 63:2; 105:4; Isaiah 6:1 and 2; Ezekiel 1:1, 26-28; 8:2-4;10:1 and 4; 43:2-7; Amos 9:1; Matthew 3:16; 5:8; John 14:21; Acts 9:10; 18:9; Hebrews 12:14

30. Exodus 19:16-19; 33:9-11 and 13-20; Deuteronomy 23:14; Numbers 6:24-26; 2 Chronicles 6:17; Job 29:3; 33:26-30; Psalm 11:7; 16:8; 17:15; 26:2-3; 27:1, 4 and 8; 31:15-16; 34:4-5; 36:9; 37:4-7; 41:4; 42:1-2; 43:3; 57:7-11; 63:1-2; 67:1; 80:3,7 and 19; 89:15; 90:8; 91:1; 97:3-6 and 11; 108:5; 119:135; Proverbs 8:17-18 and 34-35; 20:27; Isaiah 6:1-7; 9:1 and 5-6; 10:16-17; 26:3; 40:31; 60:1-3; Malachi 4:2; Matthew 3:10; 4:16; 17:2;18:9; Mark 9:47; Luke 3:9 and 16; John 1:1-5 and 9; 8:12; 14:30; Acts 7:55 and 6:15; 9:3-4; Romans 12:1-2; 1 Corinthians 6:11; 11:27-29; 2 Corinthians 3:18; 4:3-6 and 16-18; 7:1; Ephesians 4:21-24; 5:8-14; Hebrews 1:1-13; 12:29; 1 John 1:7 and 9; 3:20-21; Revelation 1:10-18; 21:23-24

31. 1 Samuel 13:13-14; Acts 13:22

32. Exodus 40:6 and 12; Deuteronomy 31:5; Psalm 51:15-17; 69:30-31; 100:2-4; John 10:9; 14:6; Hebrews 4:16; 13:11-15; Revelation 3:6-8

33. Exodus 31:13; Ezekiel 37:28; Ephesians 2:4-13; 1 Thessalonians 5:23; 2 Thessalonians 1:11-12; Jude 1:1

34. Deuteronomy 4:1-9, 13 and 40; Deuteronomy 29:9; Ezekiel 11:19-20; John 15:1-17; Hebrews 6:4-5

35. Psalm 40:8-10; 1 Thessalonians 4:7; 2 Thessalonians 3:3-4; Hebrews 13:20-21

36. Matthew 22:36-40; John 15:12; 1 Thessalonians 4:9; 1 John 3:23

37. Deuteronomy 4:40; 5:32-33; Psalm 101:2; 119:2 and 10-11; Matthew 6:22

38. Colossians 3:1-5

39. Job 42:5 and 6; John 12:25-26; Romans 8:11; Galatians 2:19-20; 5:24; 1 John 2:16

40. Isaiah 54:17; 1 Corinthians 3:16; 6:19; 2 Corinthians 3:18; 4:17-18; Ephesians 4:22-24; Hebrews 12:1-2

41. John 16:13; Romans 5:9; 8:1; 1 Corinthians 3:16; 2 Corinthians 5:7; Ephesians 3:19 (Amplified); 1 Thessalonians 5:23-24; Titus 3:5-7; 1 John 1:7and 9; 5:18

42. Psalm 25:1; Matthew 6:22; John 15:1-17; Romans 12:1- 2; 1 John 1:7

43. Exodus 25:20-25; Psalm 16:11; 2 Corinthians 4:6; Ephesians 1:17

44. Psalm 23:4; Ezekiel 48:35

45. Psalm 32:5; 90:8; 139:23-24; Hosea 10:12; Romans 12:2; 1 Corinthians 11:28; 2 Corinthians 3:18; 4:16-18; 7:1; Ephesians 4:23; Philippians 4:8; 1 Peter 1:13;

46. John 15:3; Romans 8:2 and 35-39; 2 Timothy 3:16-17; Hebrews 10:22

47. Proverbs 4:23; Matthew 15:6; 2 Corinthians 10:5

48. Job 31:1; Psalm 1:1-3; 84:10; 101:3; Isaiah 1:4-5 and 16-20; 33:14-16; Amos 5:14-15; Habakkuk 1:13; Matthew 5:27-29; 18:8-9; John 3:16-21; 14:30; Romans 7:22 through 8:2; 1 Corinthians 6:15-19; Colossians 3:1-2; 2 Timothy 2:22; Titus 2:11-14; James 4:4-7; 1 Peter 2:11-12; 1 John 2:15-17; Jude 1:1-25;

49. Psalm 19:12-14; John 14:30

50. Exodus 15:2; 1 Chronicles 16:35; Psalm 18:46; 27:9; 65:5; 91:16; Isaiah 12:2-3; 49:26; Micah 7:7; Luke 2:29-30; John 1:12; 4:14; 2 Timothy 1:9-10; Titus 2:11-14; 3:4-7; Jude 1:25

51. Matthew 16:24; John 5:39

52. Joshua 1:1-9

53. Judges 6:24; John 14:27; Hebrews 13:20-21

54. John 14:27; Romans 5:1

55. Isaiah 54:17 (Amplified); Ephesians 6:12; Philippians 1:28; 2 Timothy 1:7

56. Deuteronomy 10:12; Psalm 19:9; 29:1-11; 89:7; Hebrews 12:28 (NIV)

57. Joshua 1:6-9; Joshua 24:14-15; 1 Kings 18:21; Psalm 16:8; Proverbs 3:5-6; Jeremiah 17:5-8; Matthew 21:21

58. Psalm 67:1-3; Matthew 28:19-20; Mark 16:15 and 20; Acts 1:8; 2:36-39; 20:27; Romans 10:13-18; 2 Timothy 4:1-2; Hebrews 13:15

59. Psalm 110:1; Proverbs 8:22-30; Isaiah 9:5-6; 40:25; 41:14 and 20; 42:1-8 and 19-21; Matthew 26:63-64; 28:17-18; Mark 1:14-15; 16:19; John 1:1-14; 5:18, and 23-24, and 36-39; 8:24; 10:30-33; 14:6-11; 16:30; 20:28-31; Acts 10:38 and 42-43; 13:39 (Amplified); Romans 3:21-31; 10:8-10; 1 Corinthians 1:23-24; 6:20; 2 Corinthians 5:17-19; Philippians 2:6-11; Colossians 1:14-22; 2:9; 1 Timothy 1:15; 2:5; 3:16; 6:13-16; Titus 2:13-14; Hebrews 1:1-9; 4:14-15; 9:11-12; 1 John 3:5-8; 4:14; 5:20; Revelation 1:4-18; 12:10; 19:11-13; 21:3 and 6-7

60. Genesis 1:26-28; Psalm 8:3-6; Isaiah 7:14; Romans 8:9-11; Romans 8:11-17; 1 Corinthians 15:1-8; 2 Corinthians 5:21 (Amplified); Ephesians 1:7; 2:4-10 and 13; Philippians 2:8-10 (Amplified); Colossians 1:20 (Amplified); Hebrews 2:3; 9:12; 10:19, 20, and 22-23; 13:12; 1 John 2:2; Jude 1:20-25; Revelation 1:5-6; 3:21; 5:9-10

61. John 16:33; 2 Corinthians 5:21; 10:4; Galatians 3:13-14

62. Exodus 20:2,5 and 7; Deuteronomy 6:12; 2 Samuel 22:2; Psalm 18:2; 40:17; 144:2; Isaiah 40:1-2

63. Galatians 5:1; Ephesians 4:27; 1 Thessalonians 4:3-7; 1 Peter 2:11

64. Exodus 17:15; Joshua 5:13-14; Isaiah 13:2-4 and 11; Revelation 19:11-16

65. Joshua 10:12; 1 Samuel 1:3 and 17:45; Jeremiah 10:16; Romans 9:29

66. John 14:30; 2 Corinthians 10:4-5; James 4:7; 1 Peter 5:8-9; 1 John 4:4

67. 2 Chronicles 14:1-6; Matthew 16:19; Mark 3:27; Luke 10:18-19; Ephesians 6:12;

68. Nehemiah 4:6-9; Proverbs 25:28; Isaiah 6:8; 58:12; Ezekiel 22:25-30; Matthew 7:24-26; 1 Peter 5:8

69. Isaiah 58:10; Daniel 7:27; Matthew 10:7; Acts 26:18; Romans 8:19; Colossians 2:15; 1 Peter 2:9

70. 1 Samuel 30:8; Jeremiah 30:8, and 16-17; 2 Corinthians 5:18-20

71. Psalm 108:13; Romans 8:37; 16:20

72. Psalm 33:22; 119:41; Zechariah 14:5-7 and 9; Matthew 9:36; Romans 5:5-8; 2 Corinthians 1:3-4; 1 Peter 5:7

73. Psalm 27:4; Song of Solomon 3:3-4; John 10:27-29; 14:15-21; Romans 8:35-39

74. Proverbs 11:31; Luke 18:28-30; Revelation 1:5-6

75. Isaiah 54:17 (Amplified); 2 Corinthians 2:14

76. Isaiah 54:17 (Amplified); Ephesians 6:12; Colossians 2:15

77. Isaiah 61:1; Romans 8:1; Colossians 2:15; Hebrews 2:14-15

78. Zechariah 4:6-7; John 14:13-14; Mark 11:22-24; Romans 4:20-21

79. Deuteronomy 8:18; Nehemiah 5:11-12; 2 Corinthians 8:9

80. Deuteronomy 8:18

81. Malachi 3:10-12

82. Isaiah 14:12-17; Ezekiel 28:17-19; John 10:10; 16:33; 2 Corinthians 2:14

83. Exodus 15:25-26; Psalm 103:1-3; Isaiah 53:4-5; John 4:13-14; 1 Peter 2:24

84. Habakkuk 3:4 (Amplified); Matthew 16:19; 18:18; Luke 10:17-19; Philippians 1:28; Colossians 2:15; Revelations 12:11

85. Deuteronomy 1:11; 32:35; Job 36:7 and 11; Proverbs 11:31; Jeremiah 32:18; Romans 12:17-19; Hebrews 10:30

86. Isaiah 61:7; Zechariah 9:12

87. Proverbs 6:30-31

88. Psalm 4:1;24:3-6; ; Isaiah 54:14 and 17; Jeremiah 23:5-6; Matthew 6:33; John 17:22; Romans 3:21 and 22; 4:3-8; 1 Corinthians 1:30; 2 Corinthians 5:21; Philippians 3:9; 2 Timothy 3:1, 5-17; 2 Peter 1:1

89. Luke 10:19-20; Revelation 20:12 and 15

90. Genesis 12:2-3; 26:1-4 and 12-14; Numbers 6:25; Deuteronomy 15:6; 28:1-14; 29:9; 1 Chronicles 17:26-27; Job 10:12; Psalm 3:8; 63:3-4; 133:3; Proverbs 8:17-21;10:22

91. Genesis 32:24-30; Exodus 24:9-11; 33:11-20; Job: 19:25-27; Psalm 139:8; Ezekiel 1:26-28; Matthew 5:8; John 4:24; 14:6; Acts 7:55 and 56; Ephesians 2:4-6; Colossians 3:1; Hebrews 4:16; 9:6-14; 10:19; Revelation 4:1-11; 19:11-16

92. Exodus 24:8-10; Psalm 23:3-6; 24: 3-6; 68:18 and 19; 99:5; 100:4; 118:19 and 20; 139:8; Luke 13:24; John 3:13; Acts 10:9-11; 2 Corinthians 12:2-4; Ephesians 4:7 and 8; Philippians 4:19; Hebrews 4:16; 6:19-20; Revelation 1:10-19; 4:1-11; 21:9-27

93. Genesis 28:12-17; Psalm 78:23; Ezekiel 1:1 and 28 through 2:5; Malachi 3:10; Matthew 3:16 and 17; Mark 7:34; Luke 9:16; John 1:51; Acts 7:55 and 56; 1 Peter 1:12 and 13

94. Deuteronomy 1:8; Psalm 118:21 and 25; 144:12-15; Joel 2:25; Habakkuk 2:3; Isaiah 10:25 and 27; Ezekiel 12:25; Daniel 10:10-13; Luke 18:28-30; 1 Thessalonians 2:18; 1 Peter 1:13

95. Deuteronomy 5:25; 6:17-19 and 24; 28:1-2 and 11; 29:9; 31:8; Joshua 1:8; 2 Chronicles 26:4-5; 27:6; Psalm 84:11; 23:6; 25:14

and 21; 34:7, 9 and 10; 119:77 and 173; 133:1-3; 145:18; 17:1-3 and 15; 50: 23; 37:27-28, 34, and 37; 112:1-3; 103:20; Proverbs 8:17-18 and 34-35; 10:6; 10:24; 16:13; 22:4; 23:7; Malachi 3:10; Matthew 6:33; 7:7-11 and 16; 21:22; 18:20; 28:19-20; Mark 10:29-30; 11:22-24; Luke 6:38; John 14:15-21 and 23; 15:4; 16:23-24; 2 Corinthians 9:8; Ephesians 3:20; Hebrews 1:14; 13:5; James 1:5, 9 and 12; 4: 6, 8, 10

96. Nehemiah 1:11 (Amplified); Luke 2:52; 6:38

97. Job 27:13 and 16-17; Proverbs 13:22; Ecclesiastes 2:26; Isaiah 45:2 and 3

98. Deuteronomy 8:18; Proverbs 8:12; 25:2

99. Genesis 12:2-3; Deuteronomy 14:22-29; 16:16; Leviticus 27:30; Job 22:21-28; 36:11; Psalm 35:27; 103; 112; Proverbs 3:9; 8:17-18 and 21; Zechariah 9:12; Malachi 3:8-10; Luke 12:32; 3 John 1:2

100. Genesis 22:14; Luke 22:35

101. Psalm 23:5-6; 68:19; 71:21

102. Proverbs 10:24; 34:7; Matthew 9:29;

103. Psalm 3:3; 16:11; 43:4; 97:1; 98:4; Ecclesiastes 2:26; 3:11-13; Isaiah 61:10; Jeremiah 15:16; Galatians 5:22

104. Psalm 16:11; 37:4; 100:2; Ecclesiastes 5:18-20; Zephaniah 3:17; Matthew 25:21 and 23; 17:13; Luke 18:28-30; John 5:11; Romans 15:13; Philippians 4:4; 1 Thessalonians 5:16;

105. Nehemiah 8:10

106. Genesis 21:6; Job 5:20-22; 8:21; Psalm 13:5-6; 20:5; 30:5 and 11-12; 36:7-9; 43:4; 53:6; 68:3; 126:1-6; 146:5; Isaiah 12:3; 35:10; Jeremiah 15:16; Luke 6:21 and 23 (Amplified); John 10:10; 15:11; Acts 13:52; Romans 14:17; Revelation 5:9-10

107. Habakkuk 3:4 (Amplified); John 15:16; 9:4; Matthew 5:16; 1 Corinthians 12:7; Ephesians 2:10; Titus 2:114; Hebrews 10:24; 1 Peter 2:12

108. Matthew 6:1-4; 10:21; 19:21-22; Luke 12:21; Acts 20:35; 2

Corinthians 8:7; 9:7; 1 Timothy 6:17-19

109. Deuteronomy 1:8; Luke 10:9

110. Isaiah 9:5-6; 53:5-6; Matthew 11:28-29; Luke 22:24-30; John 1:29; 12:32; Philippians 2:5-11; 1 John 5:20

111. Matthew 13:23; John 15:1-17

112. Genesis 12:2-3; Matthew 5:16; Acts 10:1-4 and 31

113. Genesis 49:24; Deuteronomy 15:7-11; Psalm 23:1; 80:1; John 16:13; 1 Timothy 6:18;

114. Genesis 17:1; Genesis 35:11; Genesis 49:24-25; 1 Chronicles 4:10; 2 Corinthians 9:8-11; Philippians 4:19; 2 Timothy 3:17

115. Genesis 26:1-4 and 12-14; Mark 10:29-30; Luke 6:38

116. Genesis 22:17; Exodus 20:12; 23:25; Job 42:10-12; Psalm 37:3-6; Proverbs 18:21; 19:17; 22:9; Ecclesiastes 5:13-14 and 18-20; 11:1; Isaiah 58:5-14; Malachi 3:10; Matthew 5:7; 10:7-10 and 41-42; Mark 10:29-30; Luke 6:35-38; 1 Corinthians 3:8; 2 Corinthians 9:6-12; Galatians 6:9; Hebrews 6:14; 1 Peter 3:9

117. Psalm 68:5; 82:3; 146:9; James 1:27

118. Proverbs 19:17; 82:3; Matthew 25:40; James 1:27

119. Proverbs 4:23; 1 Peter 3:10

120. Psalm 19:14; 39:1; 101:2-4; 139:23-24; Proverbs 4:7; 4:23; Isaiah 58:9; Jeremiah 17:9-10; Matthew 12:33-37; Ephesians 5:3-4; Philippians 2:13-15; 4:6-7; James 3:2-12

121. Psalm 35:28; 119:171-172; Proverbs 18:21

122. Psalm 119:140; Isaiah 40:8; 45:22-23; 55:11; Malachi 3:6; Mark 11:22-24; Romans 4:20-21; 2 Corinthians 1:20; Titus 1:2; Hebrews 6:17-18; 10:23

123. Psalm 149:6; Isaiah 49:2; Ephesians 6:10-18; Hebrews 4:12; Revelations 1:16; 2:16; 11:3-6; 19:15 and 21

124. Numbers 14:20; Jeremiah 22:16; Matthew 18:32-35; Mark

11:25-26; Luke 11:4; John 20:23; Acts 7:59-60; 2 Corinthians 5:17-21; Colossians 3:12-13

125. Isaiah 61:1-3, 6-7 and 10; James 1:27

126. 2 Corinthians 2:14; 10:4-5; 1 John 3:8

127. Matthew 16:16-18

128. Genesis 1:1, 3, 6 and 9; Exodus 4:12; 7:1; 14:15-16 and 31; Joshua 1:5; 10:12-14; 1 Kings 17:24; Psalm 33:4, 6 and 9; 81:10; 119:103; Jeremiah 1:7 and 9; Ezekiel 2:1 through 3:4; 37:3-10; Isaiah 51:15-16; 57:19; 59:21; Joel 2:28; Matthew 16:19; Mark 11:22-24; John 1:12; 10:34; 15:7-8; Romans 8:16-19; 2 Corinthians 2:17; 4:7; 5:20; Ephesians 3:20; 5:1; 6:17-18; 2 Thessalonians 1:11-12; Hebrews 11:1-3; 1 Peter 2:9; 4:11

129. Job 22:28 (Amplified); Isaiah 55:11

130. Numbers 20:16; 1 Chronicles 21:15; 2 Chronicles 32:21; Daniel 3:28; 6:22; Matthew 26:53; Luke 1:26-27; Acts 12:11; Revelation 1:1; 22:6; 22:16

131. 2 Kings 6:16; Daniel 10:13; Hebrews 12:22; Revelation 5:9-12

132. Exodus 23:14, 15, 20, 22, and 25-26; Psalm 34:7-10; 91:11 and 14-15; 115:13-15; Acts 5:19-20; 12:6-11; Hebrews 1:14 (Amplified)

133. Psalm 103:20

134. 1 Samuel 3:19; Mark 11:24; John 11:40; Hebrews 11:6 ; 1 John 3:22

135. Proverbs 10:20-21; 18:21; Matthew 12:35; Romans 10:8-10

136. Job 22:28; Mark 11:22-24; John 15:7; 2 Corinthians 4:13

137. 1 Samuel 9:9; 1 Kings 18:41-45; Proverbs 23:7; Joel 2:28; Matthew 6:10 and 33; 12:35; Luke 6:45; John 5:19 and 20; 8:38; Acts 2:17; Romans 4:17; 2 Corinthians 4:16-18; Ephesians 1:17 and 18; 3:20; Philippians 4:6-8; Colossians 3:1-2; Hebrews 10:38; 11:1 and 3, and 6 and 22

138. Proverbs 4:25-27; Acts 2:17; 1 Corinthians 13:2; Hebrews 10:35; 1 John 2:5 (Amplified)

139. Luke 1:30; John 11:40; Hebrews 10:23 and 36; 2 Peter 1:2-8 (Amplified)

140. Deuteronomy 6:10-11; 8:11-14; 28:11; Hosea 4:6; Proverbs 13:11-22; Matthew 6:6; 6:33; Ephesians 1:11-12; James 4:2

141. Psalm 102:13; Isaiah 60:1; 1 Peter 2:9-12

142. Genesis 30:27; 41:43; Deuteronomy 28:13; Psalm 21:1-7; 71:21; Daniel 2:48; Matthew 5:14-16; Luke 12:32; Romans 12:6-8 and 11-13; Revelation 5:9-10;

143. Proverbs 15:6

144. Isaiah 1:17-19; 54:1-3; Zechariah 7:9-10; Matthew 18:5; James 1:27

145. Psalm 68:5 and 6; 82:3-4; Proverbs 3:27; Zechariah 7:8-10; Mark 10:29-30; John 3:17; James 1:27

146. Genesis 12:2-3; Proverbs 3:9-10

147. Luke 10:1

148. Exodus 15:25-26; Psalm 103:1-3; Isaiah 53:4-5; Habakkuk 3:4 (Amplified); Luke 10:9 and 17-19; John 4:13-14

149. 2 Samuel 7:9; 1 Chronicles 25:1-7; Psalm 33:3

150. 1 Corinthians 4:9; Romans 8:34-39; Hebrews 11:36-38; Revelation 6:9-11

151. Proverbs 11:24; Matthew 25:31-40; Luke 18:28-30; 2 Corinthians 9:8-11

152. Job 22:21-28; Isaiah 55:11; Mark 11:22-24; Hebrews 3:1

153. 1 Samuel 3:19; 1 Kings 18:36-39; 1 Chronicles 4:10; Psalm 20:4-5; Isaiah 45:11; Jeremiah 1:12; John 16:24; 1 John 5:14-15

154. John 14:10-14; Hebrews 3:1; 7:21-8:1; 10:19-23;

155. Numbers 11:23; 23:19; Matthew 6:9-10; Matthew 7:7-8 and 11; 11:12

About the Author

Louis McCall was born in Chicago, Illinois and attended Northwestern University where he received a Ph.D. Later, he also attended the National War College of the National Defense University. Louis was an Assistant Professor at the Ohio State University prior to a 36-year career in the U.S. Department of State, first as a Foreign Service officer and then as a foreign affairs Civil Service employee where he served as Consul General, Chargé d'Affaires, U.S. Representative, and Assistant Inspector General. He lived in or worked in, at least temporarily, 60 countries on six continents. Whether in academia or as a diplomat, Louis found opportunities to live his faith, including part-time ministry of the good news in word and in song, including co-laboring with missionaries, national church leaders, and the underground church. When ministering early in his diplomatic career from the pulpit of a great church in Calcutta, India, Louis said to those in attendance that he had determined not to be ashamed of the gospel of Christ. That has been a commitment he has endeavored to keep over the years. In his final two years at the Department of State he organized and led the National Day of Prayer observances in the Department.

Now, in his new career as an author, he has the pleasure of greater freedom in sharing what God has placed in his heart. Louis is active simultaneously in two churches in Washington, D.C. One is a multi-site non-denominational church and the other a Catholic church where he is a regular cantor, though not a Catholic himself. He has managed this with the blessing and full knowledge of pastors and priests. This has been an outgrowth of his early association with a mixed protestant-Catholic charismatic house-based worship group, his association with the late Mother Theresa of Calcutta, his Catholic charismatic wife, and guest ministry in churches and bible schools of various denominations while living in or working in other countries.

TO CONTACT
OR
FOLLOW THE AUTHOR

I truly hope you enjoyed this book. It was written for you. Please recommend it to others. I also welcome your feedback. It would really encourage me to hear from you. You can follow me on my website and on social media using the links below. For snail mail devotees there is also a regular mail address for you.

WEBSITE: http://www.louismccallinternational.com

Email: louismccall85@gmail.com

ADDRESS: Louis McCall International,
P.O. Box 60211,
Washington, DC 20039

GOOGLE+: https://plus.google.com/+louismccall85

Facebook: https://www.facebook.com/
louismccallinternational

TWITTER: @DrLouisMcCal
https://twitter.com/DrLouisMcCall

GOODREADS: https://www.goodreads.com/
louismccallinternational

NOTES